The Authors

E.G. Richards, MC, BSc, FICF, is a forestry and forest industries consultant and a Director of Land and Timber Services Ltd. He was formerly Director of Land Use, Forestry Commission.

J.R. Aaron, MA, MSc, FICF, FIWSc, MIHort, is a consultant in timber technology and was formerly Head of the Forestry Commission's Wood Utilisation Branch. He pioneered the use of forest bark in horticulture in the UK.

G.F. d'A. Savage, BSc, MICF, served with the Forestry Commission as a Forest District Manager in each of the countries of Scotland, Wales and England and occupied specialist posts as Education Officer in charge of Gwydyr Forester Training School, as Management Training Officer at the Forest of Dean, and as Private Woodland Officer in South West England.

M.R.W. Williams, MA, FICF, is a chartered forester and former Lecturer in Forestry at the Cumbria College of Agriculture and Forestry, Newton Rigg, Penrith. He was previously District Officer with the Forestry Commission and General Manager of a Woodland Owners Co-operative.

Trees as a Farm Crop

E.G. Richards, J.R. Aaron,
G.F. d'A. Savage and M.R.W. Williams

Illustrations by
Peter Reddy and Elsa Wood

BSP PROFESSIONAL BOOKS

OXFORD LONDON EDINBURGH
BOSTON PALO ALTO MELBOURNE

First published 1988

British Library
Cataloguing in Publication Data
Trees as a farm crop.
  1. Trees. Cultivation
  I. Richards, E.G. (Ernest Glenesk)
  634.915

ISBN 0–632–02321–X

BSP Professional Books
A division of Blackwell Scientific
  Publications Ltd
Editorial Offices:
Osney Mead, Oxford OX2 0EL
  (Orders: Tel. 0865 240201)
8 John Street, London WC1N 2ES
23 Ainslie Place, Edinburgh EH3 6AJ
3 Cambridge Center, Suite 208, Cambridge,
  MA 02142, USA
667 Lytton Avenue, Palo Alto, California
  94301, USA
107 Barry Street, Carlton, Victoria 3053,
  Australia

Set by DMD Ltd, St Clements, Oxford

Cover illustration by Peter Reddy

Printed and bound in Great Britain by
Mackays of Chatham PLC, Chatham, Kent

Contents

Acknowledgements

Thanks are due to John Birchmore and Chris Inglis, both of Land and Timber Services Ltd, Edinburgh, who gave helpful advice during the preparation of the manuscript; and to Mrs Marjorie Liston who typed the final text.

We also wish to express our appreciation to the Forestry Commission for their permission to make use of their most recent work on herbicides in Chapter 4 and to reproduce their Sales Agreements in Appendix 4. Mr J. Airlie Bruce Jones kindly provided the photographs for Figs 9.8 and 9.11.

Elsa Wood drew the illustrations in Chapter 1 and Peter Reddy drew the rest in the book, together with the cover illustration. We thank them both for their splendid work.

We also wish to thank Richard Miles, Publisher, and Caroline Savage, Processing Editor, for all their help in editing the manuscript and preparing it for the printer.

E.G. Richards
J.R. Aaron
G.F. d'A. Savage
M.R.W. Williams

Introduction

*by Lord Mackie of Benshie, CBE, DSO, DFC,
LLD, Chairman, Land and Timber Services Ltd
and Liberal Spokesman, House of Lords, on
Scottish Affairs, Agriculture and Forestry*

Increases in the efficiency of modern agriculture have resulted in
substantial over-production of food in Europe–not only within
the European Economic Community where fiscal measures
favouring farming have resulted in large surpluses, but in
countries like Sweden which has a much higher proportion of its
land under forest. Britain still imports nearly 90 per cent of its
requirements of wood and wood products at a cost (in 1987) of
over £5,000 million a year, and it is not surprising that the
question is being asked–why not grow more wood in Britain on
some of the land currently growing food that is surplus to needs?

Britain's maritime climate with its relatively wet summers
provides good growing conditions for trees. Rates of growth are
several times those in Scandinavia, one of Britain's main
suppliers of wood and wood products. Techniques have been
developed for establishing flourishing coniferous woodlands on
poor soils unsuited for most types of agriculture except extensive
pastoral farming. On other, better, soils which may still be
marginal for agriculture except with large inputs of fertilizer, a
range of broadleaves will thrive and conifers will have very high
rates of growth.

As government policies move towards a new pattern of rural
land use the case for more forestry strengthens.

What about future demand for British-grown timber?

The British forest products industry has had its ups and downs
over the past fifty years. Between the First and Second World
Wars British timber had to face cheap imports from the forest-
rich countries: Scandinavia, Russia and Canada for conifers;
southern Europe for temperate hardwoods; and the tropical rain
forests for tropical hardwoods. The creation of new large scale
plantations in Britain between the Wars and immediately after
the Second World War made possible the setting up of new wood

processing plants. Although there were–inevitably–some that failed, others have taken their place and a new generation of diverse forest products industries is now firmly established in Britain. The traditional family sawmilling industry has been modernised and is flourishing and the demand for sawlogs is on the increase. Over the past five years there has been massive new investment in pulp, paper and board mills. To survive, these mills need large amounts of British-grown timber of all kinds– broadleaves and conifers. Europe is set to continue to consume more wood than it can produce into the foreseeable future according to the latest major review of supply and demand carried out by the Economic Commission for Europe and the European Office of the Food and Agricultural Organisation (European Timber Trends Study IV).

Growing trees on the farm to produce wood for industry does not necessarily mean creating large areas of single-species coniferous plantations. Conifers obviously have their place and some upland farms may have little choice but to plant conifers because of soil and exposure but monoculture can be avoided and diversity can be achieved by careful species selection.

On more sheltered lowland farms where the soil is fertile it might be more appropriate to grow small areas of high-quality broadleaved trees such as oak, beech and ash for sale to specialist markets. Another form of forestry that can be practised on lowland farms is coppice for firewood and fencing material. Coppice also provides good cover for game.

The time-span and the inputs of resources to create high forest where conifers will take from 40 to 100 years to reach maturity and broadleaves upwards of 100 years, are very different from those involved in the creation of coppice crops, where in 20 years from the time of planting the first coppice harvest can be expected. Even shorter coppice rotations are now envisaged for species that grow very quickly in their first few years after planting to produce a dense thicket of coppice shoots that are harvested mechanically for use as a fuel–the so-called biomass crops.

The value of properly sited woodlands, copses or spinneys for game management can be very high (outweighing their value as timber producers on some lowland farms). Their value as shelter and as a landscape feature may be more difficult to quantify in money terms but it can be substantial.

The new approach by Government to grant-aid schemes for

farm forestry where in addition to a planting grant an annual grant is paid during the early years when woodlands produce no income gives an incentive hitherto lacking in all forestry grant-aid schemes. The recent (March 1988) switch of emphasis from income tax incentives–first introduced in 1916–to the much higher rates of planting grant, will also make available resources to farmers for tree planting which hitherto were channelled to those paying the top rates of income tax.

Like farming, forestry work is seasonal. There are times in the year when both men and farm tractors are idle when they could be used on forestry work. When pressures of seasonal work on farm and forest coincide the timing of forest operations is less critical, especially after trees have been established. Once established it is not critical that jobs are done in any one year; most need to be done within a five year period. Some jobs, like pruning or brashing, can be done when there is severe weather and snow on the ground. The trees themselves give shelter to those doing the work.

The desirable balance between farming and forestry will vary with each individual farm. The once tedious calculations needed to find the optimum balance from the financial point of view can now be carried out speedily on computers, to help the individual farmer decide if and how and where to invest in woodlands.

This book is intended to give farmers guidance as to which kinds of trees will grow in the conditions which prevail on their farms and what practical work is involved in planting, tending, thinning and felling woodlands. It is hoped that it will help to answer the important question–how much work can be carried out with farm labour and when is it more sensible to call in specialist contractors? In recognition of the fact that many farmers will have interests in sporting, nature conservation, landscape and amenity, these subjects are touched on throughout the book and are dealt with in separate chapters giving guidance on woodland management when these objectives have a high priority.

We live in a period of enforced changes of emphasis in the way in which farmers use their land; the planting of trees by farmers and the management of farm woodlands is an option which must be taken seriously if farmers are to continue to play their key role as guardians of our countryside from the economic, social and environmental points of view.

Mackie of Benshie

The Farm Woodland Scheme and Forestry Commission Grant Aid

There are two forms of grant aid for tree planting on the farm. There is a once and for all grant, paid by the Forestry Commission as a contribution to the actual cost of planting and establishing woodlands, whether on the farm or not. In addition, from October 1988 there is to be an annual grant for farm woodlands planted after that date, to be paid by the Ministry of Agriculture [in Scotland by the Department of Agriculture and Fisheries for Scotland (DAFS)]. Its purpose is to give farmers an annual income during the unproductive period between the time of planting and first (revenue earning) thinnings.

Following on the publication of a consultation document in March 1987, a statement of the Government's intentions was given by Baroness Trumpington in a speech to the House of Lords in October 1987 (given below). The actual details of the Farm Woodland Scheme will be announced in October 1988, but from what has already been said it is clear that the annual Farm Woodland Scheme grants will be of the following order:

Grants for arable land and grassland which has been cultivated and reseeded within the previous ten years:

£100 per hectare in the Severely Disadvantaged Areas (SDA);
£150 per hectare in the Disadvantaged Areas (DA);
£190 per hectare in the lowlands.

For planting on permanent pasture or rough grazing (unimproved land) there will be a limited amount of money available for the SDA and DA. The rate will be:

£30 per hectare.

The length of the period over which these annual grants will be payable is:

– coppice: *10 years.* 1990

- conifers and mixed woodlands with less than 50 per cent broadleaves: *20 years*.
- broadleaves (other than pure oak or pure beech) and conifer/broadleaved mixtures with more than 50 per cent broadleaves: *30 years*.
- pure oak and pure beech: *40 years*.

Authors' note:

For existing arable or grassland *less than 10 years of age* a (once only) supplement of £200 per hectare will be added to the Forestry Commission planting grant–see 'New Forestry Commission Woodland Grant Scheme' later in this chapter.

Extracts from Baroness Trumpington's Speech to the House of Lords and details of the Forestry Commission's New Woodland Grant Scheme are given below.

Extract from Baroness Trumpington's speech to the House of Lords (October 1987)

'The scheme as originally proposed would have attracted planting on to the most marginal land available in each of the three proposed zones. The point was made in response to consultation that there was a danger that this would do relatively little to reduce surpluses which is our primary objective. Many environmental organisations also expressed concern that planting of such marginal land might lead to the loss of valuable semi-natural habitats, particularly in the lowlands. The Government has therefore decided that the scheme should concentrate on so-called improved land. This would be done by restricting eligibility to arable land and grass land up to ten years old, that is, grassland which has been cultivated and reseeded within the previous ten years. Most farmers have some land of this kind.

Because such land is more productive than originally envisaged higher rates of annual payment would be justified. We are therefore proposing rates of £100 per hectare in the Severely Disadvantaged Areas, £150 per hectare in the Disadvantaged Areas and £190 per hectare in the lowlands, in respect of arable and improved land only. We shall, however, be sticking to the target of 12000 hectares a year and the overall target of 36000 over three years.

However, because there is proportionately less improved land in hill areas, and this applies particularly in Scotland and Wales, the Government has decided that, within the overall target of 36000 hectares over 3 years some 3000 hectares will be allocated for unimproved land planted in the SDA and DA. This would allow some hill farmers to plant woodlands on areas of permanent pasture or rough grazing, provided that the land had been in productive agricultural use. The rate of aid for all such planting would be £30 per hectare, as originally proposed for the SDA, recognising the minimal CAP savings that would accrue in such areas and the fact that some farmers will be able to plant in improved land and attract the £l50 rate in the DA and the £100 rate in the SDA.

All the rates of aid under the scheme would of course be reviewed from time to time in the light of relevant factors.

We are also anxious to give encouragement to mixed woodland containing a high percentage of broadleaves. Such woodland offers both silvicultural and economic benefits in some cases and can be a good way of establishing an eventual pure broadleaf plantation. We therefore propose to extend the payment period to 30 years for mixed woodland containing more than 50 per cent broadleaves. In addition, we intend to introduce an even longer payment period of 40 years for pure oak and beech planting, since these traditional species take longer to mature. The payment periods will therefore be: 40 years for pure oak and beech; 30 years for other broadleaves and for mixed woodland of which more than half is broadleaved; and 20 years for other woodland.

I should emphasise to your Lordships that the extra incentives which I have mentioned for broadleaf planting would be additional to and reinforce the higher rates of planting grant already payable for broadleaves. For a wood of three to ten hectares the planting grant under the Broadleaved Woodland Grant Scheme is currently £800 per hectare whereas the corresponding rate for conifers under the Foresty Grant Scheme is only £420 per hectare. *[In a written Parliamentary Answer on 23 March 1988 The Secretary of State for Scotland gave details of a new Forestry Commission Planting Grant Scheme–The Woodland Grant Scheme–with greatly increased levels of planting grant, reproduced later in this chapter.]*

We have also decided that the planting of new trees for traditional coppice rotation should be eligible for the scheme, provided that it qualifies for Forestry Commission planting grants. Because of the earlier returns that can be expected from coppicing, the annual payments would only continue for ten years. Shorter rotation coppice for energy uses would not be eligible.

A number of consultees urged us to impose compulsory minimum proportions of broadleaves that would apply to individual applications. We are not persuaded that such a step is necessary. It is true that in past years much of the traditional forestry planting in the United Kingdom as a whole has tended to be coniferous. But in England where most planting takes place on lower land, 64 per cent of private sector planting last year under Forestry Commission grant schemes was of broadleaved trees. We remain committed to the aim of achieving at least one third broadleaves under this scheme, and we take the view that the targeting of the scheme on better quality land and the incentives it provides for broadleaf planting will enable us to achieve this aim without compulsory minimum proportions. Moreover, sensitive planting will be encouraged in our advisory literature and the actual planting under the scheme will be closely monitored so that action can be taken if the broadleaf proportion falls short of what we expect.

On the minimum and maximum areas per holding, we now propose a maximum of 40 hectares per holding throughout the UK. The woodland will have to form part of the applicant's farming operations and so afforestation of the whole holding will be ruled out. The minimum per holding will be 3 hectares–except in Northern Ireland where the average holding size is much less and so the minimum plantation will only be l hectare per holding. The minimum size for each block of woodland will remain at l hectare: the logic of this is to ensure that farmers take sizeable pieces of land out of production.

In drawing up these proposals, we have been concerned to try and simplify the scheme as far as possible and to keep administrative costs to the minimum. To this end, we have decided to reduce the amount of consultation with local author-ities on planting of farm woodlands where small areas are involved particularly on improved land. On larger areas, perhaps of over 10 hectares, consultation continues to be appropriate because of the possible landscape implications. Existing arrangements would, however, continue in national designated areas such as Sites of Special Scientific Interest, Environmentally Sensitive Areas, National Parks in England and Wales and National Scenic Areas in Scotland. National Nature Reserves will be excluded from the scheme altogether. My Right Hon. Friend will want to discuss the details with representatives of local authorities, but change is needed to save money and speed up the processing of applications which will make the Farm Woodland Scheme more attractive.

Although, as I have said, we are concerned to keep costs down, we shall be allocating some additional manpower to this Scheme both at the Forestry Commission and within the Agriculture Departments' advisory services. For many farmers this will be their first venture into woodlands and good advice will be essential to ensure that the investment in young trees is not wasted. As for diversification, general advice from ADAS will be free, but detailed work on a project will be a chargeable service.

On the subject of young trees, the Government is particularly conscious of the need to obtain adequate supplies of nursery stock for planting under the scheme. My Department and the Forestry Commission have had a number of meetings with the Horticultural Trades Association on this subject and will be continuing to liaise closely with nursery growers. We shall be doing what we can to ensure that enough young trees are available, that they are of good quality stock and, as far as possible, supplied from domestic sources. My Lords, I am fully aware of the difficulties caused by the recent storms.

Finally, questions have been raised about landlord/tenant issues in relation to the scheme, The Government is keen that tenant farmers should be able, with their landlords' agreement, to participate in the scheme. Discussions have been taking place between representatives of the National Farmers' Union, the Country Landowners' Association and the Royal Institute of Chartered Surveyors on the best way to achieve this. We understand that agreement has been reached on all the fundamental points and that model clauses are being prepared for inclusion in tenancy agreements under the Agriculture Holdings Act and for use in model forestry leases where a separate long lease seems more sensible. The Government very much endorses this voluntary approach since agreement between landlord and tenant is sensible on a long term enterprise of this kind and we should not embark lightly on changes to the landlord/tenant legislation. This represents a careful balance of interests and, only relatively recently, was amended and debated at enormous length in Parliament. We shall, however, exclude from the scheme land that has been taken back into hand by a landlord for forestry under a tenancy agreement resumption clause.'

New Forestry Commission Woodland Grant Scheme

A new Woodland Grant Scheme to provide Government support for private forestry planting was announced on 23 March 1988 by the Rt. Hon. Malcolm Rifkind QC MP, Secretary of State for Scotland in a written Parliamentary Answer.

The Scheme will replace the Forestry Grant Scheme and the Broadleaved Woodland Grant Scheme which were closed to new applications from 15 March 1988.

The two main features of the Scheme are increases in grants for conifer and broadleaved planting, and new provisions to conserve the environment including guidelines on species, landscape, nature conservation, recreation, public access, archaeology and water.

The Secretary of State's statement was made in answer to a Parliamentary Question from Sir Hector Monro.

The full text of the Question and Answer is:

Sir Hector Monro: 'To ask the Secretary of State for Scotland if he is in a position to announce details of the new forestry grant scheme referred to in his reply of 16 March.'

Mr Malcolm Rifkind: 'In the answer I gave on 16 March to a question put by my hon Friend, the Member for Dumfries, I stated that the changes to the tax and grant arrangements announced by my Right Hon. Friend, the Chancellor of the Exchequer, were designed to provide a simpler and more widely acceptable system of support for private forestry. [See Author's note at the end of this chapter.]

The Forestry Commission's Forestry Grant Scheme and Broadleaved Woodland Grant Scheme were closed to new applications from 15 March 1988, and will be replaced on 5 April 1988 by a single grant scheme, to be known as the Woodland Grant

Scheme. The European Commission are being informed under the provisions of Article 93 of the Treaty of Rome. Applications may be made under the scheme from 5 April 1988 but cannot be approved until clearance of the scheme by the European Commission.

The scheme will apply to the establishment and restocking of broadleaved, conifer and mixed woodlands, whether by planting or by natural regeneration, and to the rehabilitation of neglected woodland under 20 years of age. It will also cover planting done under the Farm Woodland Scheme.

The objectives of the scheme are:
- to encourage timber production;
- to provide jobs in and increase the economic potential of rural areas with declining agricultural employment and few alternative sources of economic activity;
- to provide an alternative to agricultural production and thereby assist in the reduction of agricultural surpluses;
- to enhance the landscape, to create new wildlife habitats and to provide for recreation and sporting uses in the longer term;
- to encourage the conservation and regeneration of existing forests and woodlands.

The rates of grant will be increased to the levels set out in the following table:

| Area approved for planting or regeneration (hectares) | Rates of grant | |
	Conifers (£s per hectare)	Broadleaves (£s per hectare)
Area band 0.25–0.9	1005	1575
1.0–2.9	880 (505)	1375
3.0–9.9	795 (420)	1175
10 & over	615 (240)	975

Note: Figures in brackets under Conifers are the previous conifer grant rates which will continue to apply to conifers planted under a Farm Woodland Scheme (areas of less than one hectare are not eligible for a FWS grant).

These rates of grant are generally £375 per hectare higher than those under the Forestry Grant Scheme and the Broadleaved Woodland Grant Scheme, but the increase for broadleaved trees planted or regenerated in mixed woodlands will be substantially larger.

The rates of grant for conifer planting done under the Farm Woodland Scheme will remain unchanged [see Table above]; broadleaved planting under that Scheme will, however, be eligible for the new broadleaved grants.

For new planting on existing arable or improved grassland of less than 10 years of age which is undertaken outside the Farm Woodland Scheme, there will be a supplement of £200 per hectare.

Apart from the increased rates of grant and the special supplement for planting on better land, the scheme will have a number of important features:

- the simplicity of a scheme which replaces two schemes with different conditions, and which covers all forms of planting, regeneration and rehabilitation of woodlands;
- a substantial differential in favour of broadleaves;
- all broadleaved planting, whether it be on its own or in mixture, will attract the same rates of grant;
- the broadleaved rate of grant will also apply to the planting and natural regeneration of native pinewoods in specified areas of Scotland;
- environmental objectives and provisions that will apply to all types of woodland;
- all types of natural regeneration will now be eligible for the first instalment of grant-aid at the time the preparatory work is carried out;
- grants for the rehabilitation of derelict woodlands under 20 years of age will now include conifer and mixed woodlands;
- grants will be paid in three instalments over 10 years. For conifers as well as for broadleaves, the second and third instalments will attract the rates of grant applicable when they fall due;
- grant bands will be determined by the total of the areas approved for planting or regeneration in each separate block or wood within the 5-year plan period. [June 1988 text.]

The scheme will encompass a wide range of management objectives designed not only to provide timber but also to encourage the development of multi-purpose woodland management, to achieve a proper balance between broadleaves and conifers, to enable forestry to play its full part as an alternative use of agricultural land no longer needed for food production, and to ensure that the expansion of forestry takes place in harmony with other land uses and the environment.

In this connection, applications relating to the establishment and restocking of broadleaved woodland will be subject to the provisions of the Guidelines for the Management of Broadleaved Woodland published by the Forestry Commission, and the new scheme will incorporate similar guidelines for the management of all types of woodland. These will be subject to the review of our broadleaves policy which is due to take place later this year.

Full details of the new Woodland Grant Scheme are set out in a Forestry Commission leaflet [Woodland Grant Scheme (23 March 1988)], copies of which have been placed in the Library of the House. [The Woodland Grant Scheme leaflet was revised in June 1988 in respect of some important details. The leaflet of 23 March 1988 is no longer valid nor available.]

I am sure the announcement of this new scheme, with its greatly improved rates of grant and wide-ranging objectives, will serve to underline the Government's commitment to the sensitive yet vigorous expansion of forestry.'

Authors' note

The changes to the tax arrangements for forestry announced in the March 1988 Budget took forestry out of the tax system. The main feature is that it is no longer possible to offset the cost of establishing and maintaining commercial woodlands against an owner's other income through Schedule D provisions and later on in the life of a woodland, when it becomes revenue earning, to switch to Schedule B, paying no tax on the income from the woodland, but only a relatively small amount based on the notional value of the land in its unimproved state.

1 Which Trees to Grow?

It is of fundamental importance to decide at the very outset what are the objectives of any forestry scheme. The purpose for which the trees are to be grown will make all the difference to the choice of species to be planted or regenerated. There will almost always be one or two main objectives and a number of subsidiary ones.

The objectives may include one or more of the following:

- timber production for bulk markets (e.g. pulpwood);
- timber production for sawlogs;
- timber production for local sales (e.g. fencing material);
- timber for use on the farm, including firewood;
- shelter for stock and crops;
- amenity and landscaping;
- sporting and recreation;
- nature conservation;
- cash-crops (e.g. Christmas trees).

In order to qualify for planting grants, the objectives have to be agreed with the body making the grant, i.e. the Forestry Commission or the Countryside Commission (through a Local Authority) for small groups or individual amenity trees. Detailed guidance on the choice of objectives and making a farm woodland plan to achieve them is given in Chapter 17.

Land available

Whether it will be feasible to grow the sort of trees that will most readily meet the objectives chosen will depend on the type of ground available for planting.

Most farmers will wish first to plant up their less productive land. Often this is the land that has been most recently brought into cultivation or reclaimed or improved for grazing. Old Ordnance Survey maps may be of help in showing if any farmland was formerly woodland and therefore inherently less fertile and not brought under cultivation in days of less intensive farming. This method is not of course infallible as some coppices were sited on highly productive land simply to have near the house and steading a source of fuel and leaves and twigs for animal fodder in winter. Other, usually small, woodlands owed their situation to the sporting interests of the owner or to their role as shelter belts, and these and other criteria, like landscape, may over-ride other considerations in the choice of new areas for planting.

Arable soils will grow most of the broadleaves and conifers commonly planted in Britain although conifers do not like too much lime and on chalk or limestone some (e.g. Scots pine) should be avoided since they will suffer from 'chlorosis' and become moribund. Existing trees growing on the edges of fields are often a good indicator of what will grow well.

Moist fertile soils are suitable for broadleaves and will grow conifers.

Upland, acid soils, frequently used for rough grazing are predominantly suited to conifers but will grow a limited range of broadleaves, such as birch.

An important inhibiting factor to tree growth in Britain is exposure, sometimes limiting the choice to a few species such as sycamore or Sitka spruce which stand up to exposure well. Rainfall can be critical for Sitka spruce and Japanese larch which will not thrive on less than about 800 mm annual rainfall and which prefer 900 mm or more.

Hedgerow trees

Hedgerow trees can provide a substantial volume of useful timber as well as fulfilling their important roles in the landscape and nature conservation.

The traditional species are ash, oak, sycamore and wild cherry (gean). Elm is no longer a practical possibility due to the continuing prevalence of Dutch Elm Disease.

Hedgerow trees can arise naturally in established hedges from self sown seed and these are to be preferred to growth from shoots arising from laid stems. Hedgerow trees can also be of coppice origin where self sown trees or the original tree components of a hedge have been cut over during hedge maintenance. They can be planted in the normal way provided that they are protected from stock and possibly rabbits and deer (planted trees are often more vulnerable than those that grow up inside the protection of the hedge).

Choice of trees for planting in hedgerows, methods of planting and after-care follow the general guidelines for woodlands.

Notes on common British forest trees

A *permeable* timber will absorb wood preservatives. A *resistant* timber is one that is difficult to treat with wood preservatives. A *perishable* timber will decay rapidly in situations favouring rot, e.g. in contact with the ground. A *durable* timber is resistant to decay.

The trees most commonly found in British woodlands or planted for timber production are:

Conifers	*Broadleaves*
Douglas fir	Alder
Larch	Ash
–European	Beech
–Japanese	Birch
–hybrid (Dunkeld)	Cherry
Pine	Hazel
–Scots	Hornbeam
–Corsican	Lime
–lodgepole	Oak–sessile and pedunculate
Spruce	Poplar
–Norway (European)	Sweet chestnut
–Sitka	Sycamore
Western hemlock	Willow

These trees and the less commonly found grand and silver firs and western red cedar are briefly described below.

Broadleaved species

Alder (*Alnus* spp. mainly *A. glutinosa*)

Grows in wet conditions which no tree other than willow will tolerate. Very rapid growth. Coppices freely. Once much used for making clogs and for charcoal for making gunpowder; good quality logs sometimes purchased by turneries.

Permeable; when treated with a preservative is suitable for fencing and estate work.

Ash (Fraxinus excelsior)

An exacting species which demands good calcareous loams, moist but well drained. (If you can smell wild garlic on a site ash will grow on it.) Benefits from shelter. Avoid frost hollows. The timber has a high resistance to shock loading so it is first choice for vehicle framework, tool handles and sports goods. A prime turnery furniture and veneer timber. Well grown ash is sought after by timber merchants and commands good prices. Coppices well. Poles (often coppice-grown) are cleft for fencing rails. Permeable.

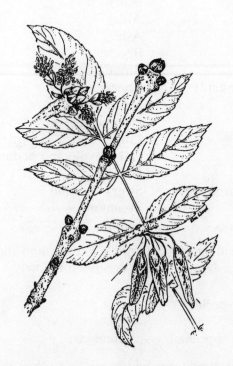

Fig. 1.1 Ash *(Fraxinus excelsior).*

Beech (Fagus sylvatica)

Native to continental Europe, though long-established in and perhaps native to Southern Britain. Tolerant of shade so used for under-planting. A suitable tree for dry limestone or chalky soils–particularly in the Cotswolds and Chilterns–but likes loams of all types if well drained. Originally it was the mainstay of the furniture industry at High Wycombe. Beech plywood from this area was used for the Mosquito bombers during the 1939–45 war. A wider range of uses indoors than any other British grown broadleaved timber. Strong, nails and screws well. Stains well. Uses include furniture; flooring; turnery (e.g. small tool handles); veneers. Permeable.

Fig. 1.2 Beech *(Fagus sylvatica).*

Birch (Betula spp.)

Birch occurs naturally all over Britain and it will tolerate acid soils. Although it will often seed naturally–and in profusion–it is difficult to establish by planting because the very fine rootlets dry out very quickly after plants have been lifted in the nursery and are in transit to the planting site. To overcome this problem birch is being grown in small tubes and the seedlings planted out, still in their tubes. They may also be grown in paper pots in which they are also planted out. There is a big variation in the vigour, early rate of growth and straightness of stem in birch. Strains of birch which have been selected for these desirable characteristics are available from specialist nurserymen. An excellent firewood.

Fig. 1.3 Birch *(Betula pendula)*.

Fig. 1.4 Birch *(Betula pubescens)*.

Cherry (Prunus avium) (= wild cherry or gean)

Likes a fertile woodland soil especially one over chalk. Has moderate strength properties. Works well and finishes well. A good joinery, furniture and turnery wood. Resistant to penetration by wood preservatives.

Fig. 1.5 Cherry *(Prunus avium)*.

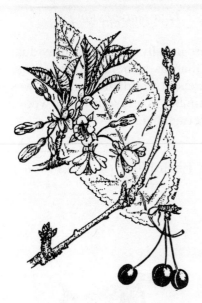

Fig. 1.6 Hazel *(Corylus avellana)*.

Hazel (Corylus avellana)

Hazel is now rarely planted to form coppice either pure or in mixture with oak standards. There is however still a limited demand for thatching spars and for hazel for cleaving for hurdles, and in Southern England a few hazel coppices are still worked in the traditional way.

Hornbeam (*Carpinus betulus*)

Hornbeam prefers fertile loams and heavier clays. It is unsuitable for acid sandy soils and high exposure. An excellent firewood but otherwise the timber is not much in demand nowadays.

Lime (*Tilia cordata : Tilia vulgaris : Tilia platyphyllos*)

The limes need fertile soils. They are usually planted as individual hedgerow or avenue trees rather than as woodland trees. Lime occurs as a natural constituent of ancient woodland, where it was usually managed as coppice. The timber is a favourite for wood-carving and is good for turnery. Permeable.

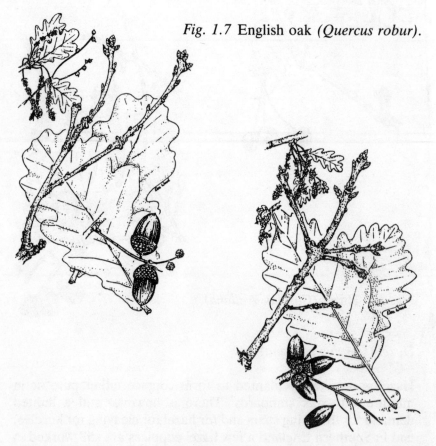

Fig. 1.7 English oak *(Quercus robur).*

Fig. 1.8 Sessile or durmast oak *(Quercus petraea).*

Oak (*Quercus robur* = pedunculate = English oak and *Quercus petraea* = sessile or Durmast oak)

Both species are native to Britain. The pedunculate or English oak grows naturally in the southern part of Britain, while the sessile or durmast oak grows in northern and western Britain. They need good loamy soils to grow well–in fact, the best oak grows on the best arable land. They will grow on *fertile* heavy soils and marls but are likely to develop cracks or 'shakes' in the timber on dry or stony sites. They are grown on a rotation of up to 150 years or longer. The timber is hard but cleaves satisfactorily. The heartwood has outstanding resistance to decay (more than 20 years life in contact with the ground). The sapwood is perishable but permeable (heartwood is extremely resistant). A prime furniture and veneer timber. Cleft oak posts and rails are a traditional fencing material in parts of England and Wales.

Poplar (*Populus* spp.)

There are many different species of poplar, including many hybrids. Poplar growing is a specialised business and professional advice must be sought (e.g. to receive Forestry Commission grants strains certified as canker-resistant must be used).

Formerly used for matches in the UK. Has a high resistance to abrasion and does not splinter–used for floors of waggons. Has low flammability and used for oast houses where the fire risk is high. Markets are currently very poor. Resistant to penetration by wood preservatives.

Sweet chestnut (*Castanea sativa*)

Needs a deep fertile soil and a mild climate. Large trees are susceptible to shake. Coppices well. Has a high proportion of durable heartwood even in quite small-diameter young material so is an excellent fencing material. Used as hop poles. Sawn-wood is good for external joinery (e.g. window frames, glazing bars) and for furniture.

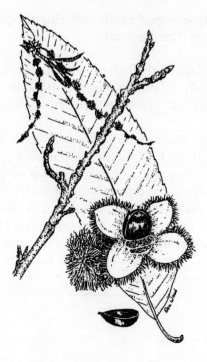

Fig. 1.9 Sweet chestnut *(Castanea sativa)*.

Sycamore (*Acer pseudoplatanus*)

Introduced from Europe, possibly by the Saxons. Stands exposure and industrial smoke pollution very well. Grey squirrels can be very harmful. The clean colour of the timber and its absence of smell make it the preferred species for use in contact with food, e.g. chopping blocks, kitchen implements. Used for textile rollers and in turnery and for veneers (if the grain shows 'figure' it is especially valuable). Permeable. Can be used for estate purposes if treated with a preservative.

Willow (*Salix* spp.)

The only species grown for its timber is the cricket bat willow (*Salix alba var. coerulea*) which needs alluvial or a similar fertile soil beside flowing water. Professional advice must be sought if it is decided to grow this timber.

Coniferous species

Douglas fir (Pseudotsuga menziesii)

From Western North America. Likes a well-drained deep soil of moderate fertility; grows extremely well in sheltered valley slopes. Unsuitable for exposed situations and badly drained soils. When pressure-treated with a preservative the timber is suitable for fencing and general estate work. A satisfactory construction and joinery timber.

Fig. 1.10 Douglas fir *(Pseudotsuga menziesii)*.

European larch (Larix decidua = L. europaea)

Native to continental Europe but long established in Britain. A strong light demander which is exacting in its site requirements–prefers moist well-drained loams of moderate fertility. The timber is heavier, harder, stronger and more durable than most other conifers commonly grown in Britain and this has given the species a prime place as a fencing and general estate timber. However if sapwood is present in any quantity then it should be treated with a preservative under pressure (it is resistant to treatment) when it can give a life of over 25 years in contact with the ground. Mature, selected, larch is used for boat building–for example, for the skin (planking) of the traditional Scottish fishing boat.

Fig. 1.11 Japanese larch *(Larix kaempferi).*

Japanese larch (Larix kaempferi)

Thrives over a wide range of conditions but prefers a high rainfall. The faster grown timber is of rougher quality than European larch. Young trees have a high proportion of sapwood and are unsuitable as fence posts unless pressure-treated with a preservative. A major use is for panel fencing.

Hybrid larch (European × Japanese) (Larix × eurolepis)
(= Dunkeld larch)

The natural cross first occurred at Dunkeld in Scotland. The
offspring of natural and artificial cross-pollination are variable in
that they can exhibit characteristics intermediate between the two
parents or can behave much like the European or the Japanese
parent. Some first generation hybrids from particular selected
parents are outstanding. The timber resembles that of European
larch.

Scots pine (Pinus sylvestris)

One of the three conifers native to Britain (the others being yew
and juniper). Relatively slow-growing but is adaptable to a wide
range of conditions, including dry heather sites and sandy soils.
Very frost-hardy. Not suitable for chalk or limestone soils and
high rainfall moorland. The timber is the 'redwood' of the
imported timber trade. Is a good fencing and general estate
timber. Used indoors for many purposes including construction
joinery and furniture. Permeable.

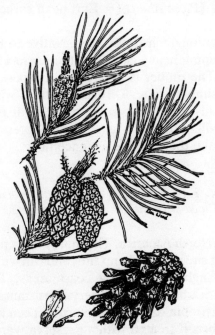

Fig. 1.12 Scots pine *(Pinus sylvestris).*

Corsican pine (*Pinus nigra var calabrica*)

Introduced from Corsica. In low elevations in the Midlands and South and East England. Grows on a wide range of soils from sands to heavy clays. Does better on chalky soils than Scots pine. Timber similar to but coarser than Scots pine and with a higher proportion of sapwood. Permeable.

Lodgepole pine (*Pinus contorta*)

From Western North America; used by the Indians for their traditional 'lodges'. Succeeds where many other trees fail. There are many different provenances and professional advice should be sought before choosing one. Some provenances produce trees with swept butts or crooked stems but where stems are straight the timber is similar to Scots pine in its range of uses. Permeable.

Norway spruce (*Picea abies*) (= European spruce)

This is the traditional Christmas tree. Native to Europe it likes a moist site including heavy clays and the less-acid peats. Dislikes heather sites. The timber is the general purpose 'whitewood' of the imported timber trade. Difficult to treat with preservatives and not naturally durable so seldom used out of doors. Young round poles will, however, take enough preservative in their sapwood to make them usable as fence posts.

Sitka spruce (*Picea sitchensis*)

From Western North America. The most widely planted conifer in Britain on poor sites. Likes damp sites and will withstand exposure and thrive in high rainfall west coast areas. Timber used for construction work but not for joinery. Resistant to impregnation with preservatives but like Norway spruce it can be used for small round fence posts if treated with a preservative.

Fig. 1.13 Sitka spruce *(Picea sitchensis).*

Silver firs (Abies alba = European silver fir; *Abies grandis*
=grand fir; *Abies procera* = noble fir)

The European silver fir is not planted in Britain due to its
susceptibility to insect damage. Grand fir from Western North
America is more resistant to the butt rot (*Fomes annosus*) than
Sitka or Norway spruce, western red cedar and the larches. It
likes a deep, well-drained soil. Stands shade so is useful for
underplanting. The timber is similar to spruce but is easier to
impregnate with preservatives. There is no provision for its use as
a structural timber in Building Regulations. Noble fir is similar to
grand fir in its site requirements but stands exposure well (grand
fir does not).

Western hemlock (Tsuga heterophylla)

From Western North America. A strong shade-bearer. Prone to
butt rot from *Fomes annosus* and *Armillaria mellea*. Tolerant of a

Table 1.1

Soil type	Broadleaved species		Conifer	
	Sheltered	Exposed	Sheltered	Exposed
Loams (Brown earth)	Most	Sycamore	Most	Sitka spruce
Podsols and other sandy soils	Birch	–	Scots pine Corsican pine Sitka spruce Larches	Sitka spruce
Iron pans	Birch	–	Sitka spruce in mixture with Lodgepole or Scots pine or a larch	
Lowland gleys	Oak Alder Birch	–	Norway spruce Corsican pine Western red cedar	
Upland gleys; peaty soils	Birch Alder Oak–where non-peaty	–	Sitka spruce or Norway spruce	Sitka spruce
Peats	Birch	–	Sitka spruce	
Calcareous soils	Beech Norway maple Sycamore Wild cherry/Gean	Sycamore	Corsican pine Lawson's cypress Western red cedar	Corsican pine

Remarks:

Podsols and other sandy soils:
   On heather plant Sitka spruce in mixture with Scots pine or a larch. Heather should be controlled with herbicide.

Lowland gleys:
   Provenance of Corsican pine important. Not suitable for northern and western Britain.

Calcareous soils:
   As for Lowland gleys.

Exposed sites in low rainfall areas:
   Plant Corsican pine in South Britain and lodgepole pine in North Britain. Sitka spruce and Japanese larch prefer a rainfall over 35 inches (900 mm).

Peats:
   Lodgepole pine may be mixed with Sitka spruce.

wide range of climatic conditions and soils. A general purpose timber. Requires to be treated under pressure if used as fence posts and pressure treatment is recommended if it is used for general estate work out of doors.

Western red cedar (Thuja plicata)

From Western North America. A strong shade bearer. Will grow on rather shallow moderately fertile soils and fairly heavy clays. Succeeds on chalk. The heartwood of this rather light-weight timber is naturally durable and is suitable for weatherboarding, greenhouses, sheds and seed boxes. Imported roofing shingles from Canada are made from selected grades of old mature WRC.

N.B. In addition to the uses listed above, which relate to farm and estate work, the thinnings of most conifers and many broadleaves are used for pulp and board manufacture in Britain. Mills processing broadleaves are located mainly in Southern Britain.

Quick guide to species choice

The quick guide to species choice is mainly of use for new planting on bare land and it should help to select the species which will grow on various types of site (Table 1.1). It can be further refined by looking at the short list of productive species to find those that are in regular demand and, where conservation is an objective, the list of native species.

Native trees and shrubs

Where nature conservation is the main or an important subsidiary objective, consideration must be given to the use of truly native tree species. These are as follows.

Native trees that produce commercial timber

Conifers
Pine (Scots)   *Pinus sylvestris*
Yew   *Taxus baccata*

Broadleaves
Alder   *Alnus glutinosa*
Ash   *Fraxinus excelsior*
Aspen   *Populus tremula*

Birch (downy)	*Betula pubescens*
(silver)	*Betula pendula*
Beech	*Fagus sylvatica*
Cherry (wild)	*Prunus avium*
Elm (Wych)	*Ulmus glabra*
Elm (English)	*Ulmus procera*
Hornbeam	*Carpinus betulus*
Lime (large leaved)	*Tilia platyphyllos*
(small leaved)	*Tilia cordata*
Oak (common)	*Quercus robur*
(sessile)	*Quercus petraea*

N.B. Sycamore (*Alder pseudoplatanus*) and Sweet Chestnut (*Castanea sativa*) although long established in Britain are not true native species, having been introduced by man.

Native trees that do not produce commercial timber

Apple (crab)	*Malus sylvestris*
Box	*Buxus sempervirens*
Cherry (bird)	*Prunus padus*
Hawthorn	*Crataegus monogyna*
Holly	*Ilex aquifolium*
Maple (field)	*Acer campestre*
Poplar (black)	*Populus nigra var betufolia*
Rowan	*Sorbus aucuparia*
Service tree (wild)	*Sorbus torminalis*
Thorn (Midland)	*Crataegus laevigata*
Whitebeam	*Sorbus aria*
Willow (bay)	*Salix pentandra*
(crack)	*Salix fragilis*
(goat)	*Salix caprea*
(white)	*Salix alba*

Coppice

Hazel	*Corylus avellana*

Short list of productive species in regular demand

Out of the wide choice of species that will give saleable timber in Britain there are a few which are used most commonly. The coniferous species with relatively high rates of growth and which produce wood which is always in demand by one or more of the major wood using industries, are, in alphabetical order:

Conifers

Corsican pine
Douglas fir
Larch (European, Japanese or hybrid [Dunkeld])
Norway spruce
Scots pine
Sitka spruce

Lodgepole pine is used on very poor sites where Sitka spruce will not thrive or as a nurse species in mixture with Sitka spruce.

In the forest-rich Nordic countries the two native species of conifer, Scots pine and Norway spruce, account for virtually all the timber grown; they have an annual rate of growth that averages about 7 cubic metres (about 7 tonnes) per hectare–Yield Class 7 in British terminology. The faster growing conifers in Britain with its milder maritime climate will achieve rates three times this figure on the best sites; the average is twice that of the Nordic countries, i.e. around 14 cubic metres per hectare per year (Yield Class 14). The only native coniferous tree, the Scots pine, is one of the slowest growing of the commonly planted conifers, often achieving only Yield Class 7 or 8 and for this reason where the climate is not too cold, Corsican pine, with 1½ times this rate of growth on comparable sites, is often preferred.

Broadleaves

Rates of growth of most native broadleaves, even on the most fertile sites, are much less than conifers and the high prices paid for their high quality furniture and joinery timbers, and for the veneer butts occasionally encountered, does not compensate for their poor productivity. But factors other than straightforward

productivity and theoretical long-term financial profitability will
weigh heavily with many woodland owners so that at least a
proportion of their woodlands will be of broadleaves, pure or in
mixture with conifers. The higher rate of planting grant for pure
broadleaves and the longer period of annual grant payment under
the Farm Woodland Scheme are also incentives that will appeal
to farmers.

The most commonly planted broadleaves are oak and beech,
both native species, and both with a wide range of uses; they are
the bread and butter species of most hardwood sawmills. Ash,
another native, is very demanding as to site but where it is at
home it grows fast and is always in demand. For coppice the first
choice must be sweet chestnut in southern Britain as, unlike
hazel, it produces timber substantial enough for fencing posts and
rails and with high natural durability; it is non-native and so not
so well regarded from the nature conservation point of view as
hazel.

A short list of broadleaves must also include two natives–the
wild cherry *Prunus avium* and birch *Betula* spp.–which are not
long-lived by broadleaved standards but which are fast-growing in
their youth. Wild cherry produces an excellent timber; it is best
planted in drifts, small groups of a few trees or even as individual
trees, in a matrix of other broadleaves. Birch should be accepted
on the same terms if it seeds in naturally. It is difficult to establish
by planting because its fine root hairs dry out so easily; seedlings
grown in small plastic tubes (not to be confused with tree
shelters) are the best answer especially for weed-free sites such as
peats. The demand for birch timber in Britain is uneven but it is
an excellent firewood.

Shade bearers and light demanders

Trees that have the ability to grow in the shade of the forest are
called shade bearers because they will *tolerate* shade; but this
does not mean that they will not grow well in full light. On the
other hand, trees classified as light demanders need a lot of light
to grow well and will be unhappy if grown in shade.

A number of species fall somewhere in between.

It is perhaps important to recognise the stronger shade bearers,
as these are the only species that will succeed well if planted in

strong shade among other, perhaps well-established, trees. It is also necessary to know which species are strong light demanders and will not thrive as forest trees if planted in shade.

Table 1.2 classifies some commonly occurring species into *strong* shade bearers and *strong* light demanders.

Table 1.2

Broadleaves		Conifers	
Strong shade bearers	Strong light demanders	Strong shade bearers	Strong light demanders
Beech	Oaks	Silver firs	Larches
		Western hemlock	Pines
		Western red cedar	
Hornbeam	Ash		
Holly	Poplar		

Other broadleaves that can be used for planting in shade in woodlands although not so strong shade bearers as the species listed above, include sycamore, Norway maple and lime.

Other conifers that will tolerate some shade in their early years include Norway spruce and Douglas fir.

2 Preparing Land for Planting

Young plantations must be fenced against farm stock, rabbits and deer, if these are prevalent, or the plants must be individually protected. Under Forestry Commission grant schemes there is no rigid specification for plantation fences. If there is a possibility of getting a grant under an agricultural scheme or from or through a Local Authority because the fence serves other purposes than protecting the plantation, then it must meet the specification required by the Agricultural Department or Local Authority.

The Forestry Commission recommend spring steel wire, because by using it the number of stakes in the fence is reduced. It needs some special tools and special techniques, and many people still prefer mild steel wire.

The sizes quoted below are given in the units commonly used, viz. Imperial sizes for woodwork and metric for wire and netting. Where appropriate the metric or Imperial equivalents are shown in brackets.

Fencing

Stock and rabbit fencing

A cheap minimum specification stock fence is (Fig. 2.1):

Straining posts: 5 inches × 7 feet (130 mm × 2.13 m) at intervals of not more than 100 m, and at corners and changes of direction.
Struts to straining posts: 4 inches × 6 feet (100 mm × 1.82 m).
Stakes (stobs): 3 inches × 5 feet 6 inches (75 mm × 1.67 m) at intervals of 3 m.
Netting: Woven field netting (pig netting) 900 mm wide (36 inches).
Wire: Two barbed wires, one at the centre of the netting and one 75 mm (3 inches) above the top of the netting.

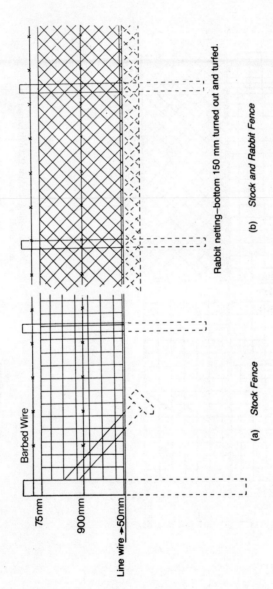

Rabbit netting—bottom 150 mm turned out and turfed.

(b) *Stock and Rabbit Fence*

(a) *Stock Fence*

Fig. 2.1 (a) Stock fence. (b) Stock and rabbit fence.

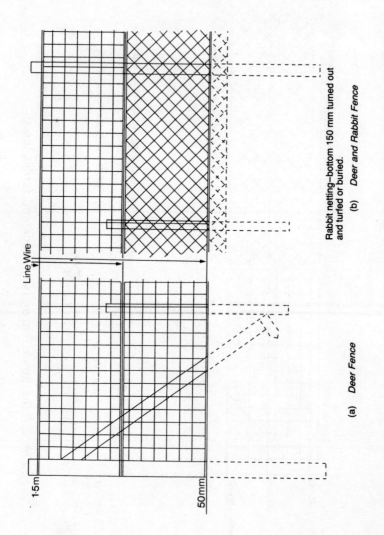

Line Wire

1·5m

50mm

Rabbit netting—bottom 150 mm turned out
and turfed or buried.

(a) *Deer Fence*

(b) *Deer and Rabbit Fence*

Fig. 2.2 (a) Deer fence.   (b) Deer and rabbit fence.

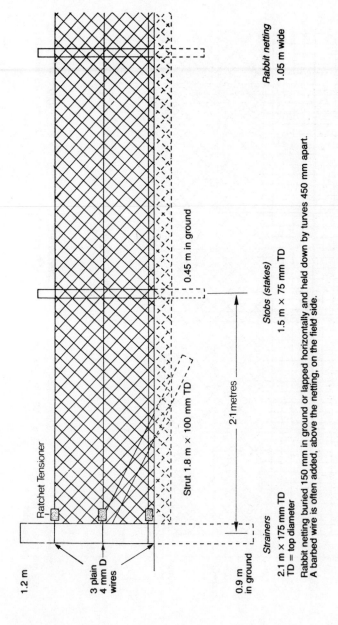

Fig. 2.3 Minimum specification stock and rabbit fence− 3 plain wires and rabbit netting (crofting counties, Scotland).

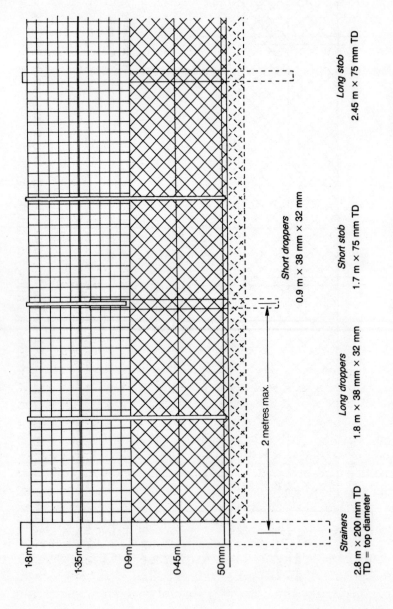

Fig. 2.4 Deer fence with rabbit netting (crofting counties, Scotland).

To make this fence rabbit-proof, use 31 m mesh galvanised 2-ply 1.25 mm netting 1050 mm (41 inches) wide instead of woven field netting. The bottom 150 mm (6 inches) must be buried in the ground or else turned outwards and held down by turfs. The rabbit netting must be supported by 8 gauge wires (metric size 4.00) at the top and 50 mm (2 inches) above ground level.

If only rabbits are to be kept out, the barbed wires are not needed and lighter stakes could be used e.g. 2–3 inches × 5 feet (50–75 mm × 1.52 m).

Deer fencing

Stock or rabbit-proof fences (Fig. 2.2) must be heightened to keep deer out. The specification given above can be altered using straining posts 5 inches × 9 feet (120 mm × 2.74 m), and struts 4 inches × 8 feet (100 mm × 2.44 m). Every third stake is replaced by one 3 inches × 8 feet 6 inches (75 mm × 2.59 m).

A second tier of woven field netting is hung above the first, supported on two 8 gauge line wires (metric size 4.00) at the top and bottom of the netting. If the fence is not required to withstand cattle, the barbed wires are not needed, but the bottom of the netting should be tied to an 8 gauge line wire 50 mm (2 inches) above ground level.

Woven field netting comes in rolls 50 m long, and rabbit netting in rolls 50 m or 25 m long. Barbed wire comes in reels 200 m long. Standard metric size 4.00 mild steel wire contains 1018 metres per 100 kg. Wire and netting are fixed to posts and stakes with 40 mm galvanised staples. Netting is fastened to line wires with tying wire or netting clips. All woodwork should be preservative-treated unless the fence is only temporary (i.e. less than 5 years).

Tradition and experience based on local conditions influence fencing specifications. The Scottish Highlands stock and rabbit fence and the deer fence shown in Figs. 2.3 and 2.4 differ in detail from those shown in Figs. 2.1 and 2.2 which are based on lowland specifications. The importance of checking on the exact specification required for grant-aided fencing is shown in Table 2.1 which illustrates the small but significant differences between two fencing specifications for the same general type of fence. It is also important to note that the lengths of straining or other posts may be given as *minimum* lengths and may need to be increased for a particular design of fence; for example, the 2.4 metres specified

Table 2.1

Type of fence			Minimum TD		Length (minimum)		
			ins	mm	Feet	ins	Metres
Stock and rabbit	A	Strainers	5	(130)	7		(2.13)
(mild steel wire)		Stakes (stobs)	3	(75)	5	6	(1.67)
	B	Strainers	(6.75)	175	(6	10)	2.1
		Stobs (stakes)	(3)	75	(5	–)	1.5
		British Standard 1722 Part 2 accepts strainers of 120 mm top diameter and intermediate posts of 60 mm top diameter.					
Deer and stock		Strainers	5	(120)	9	–	(2.74)
and/or rabbit	A	Stakes (stobs)	3	(75)	8	6	(2.59)
(mild steel wire)		Stakes (stobs)	3	(75)	5	6	(1.67)
		Strainers	(6.5)	200	(9	2)	2.8
	B	Stobs (stakes)	(3)	75	(7	10)*	2.4*
		Stobs (stakes)	(3)	75	(5	6)	1.7
		* Needs to be 8 feet and 2.45 metres for most fences.					

Figures in brackets are Imperial or metric equivalents of those in the specification.
A is extracted from a general specification.
B is extracted from a specification used for grant-aided fencing in Highland Scotland.

for long stobs for woven wire deer fences is just 50 mm (2 inches) too short for the fence illustrated; if driven to the required depth in the ground the top wire would be at the top of the post with no allowance for stapling.

British Standards

Guidance on the construction of permanent fences is given in British Standard 1733. This is published in 13 parts which are frequently revised; the following are relevant to the use of locally grown wood:

Part 1: 'Chain Link Fences'
Part 2: 'Woven Wire Fences'
Part 3: 'Strained Wire Fences'
Part 4: 'Cleft Chestnut Pale Fences'
Part 5: 'Close Boarded Fences'
Part 6: 'Wood Palisade Fences'
Part 7: 'Post and Rail Fences'
[The parts omitted concern woven-wood or steel fences.]

The Standard includes detailed recommendations on the minimum sizes of fence components, the desirability of preservative treatment, suitable wood preservatives and the method of erecting. The Forestry Commission also publish a practical guide to post and wire fences suitable for excluding rabbits, stock or deer from woods (Leaflet 87: *Forest Fencing*).

Hedges

A well maintained live hedge, especially if it be on a bank and reinforced on the field (i.e. stock) side with two strands of barbed wire on sound wooden posts, is an acceptable and aesthetically pleasing form of stock fence. It will be neither rabbit- nor deer-proof so that regeneration or planting within the wood will need to be protected by temporary fences, tree guards or shelters. Grant aid is sometimes available locally to maintain hedges (contact the Countryside Commission or National Park authority or the Agricultural Department).

Tree shelters and tree guards

Tree shelters

Tree shelters which are described under methods of planting give complete protection against rabbits and some protection against deer. They are cheaper than fencing in small areas of up to one or two hectares.

Individual tree guards for forest trees

There are a number of proprietary tree guards on the market which will protect trees from deer or rabbit browsing.

The cheapest, most commonly seen and widely used is the spiral tree guard which fits round the stem of the plant. It is suitable only for preventing bark stripping by rabbits on plants with a stem diameter in excess of 25 mm.

Plastic mesh tree guards are effective in protecting trees against bark stripping and browsing by rabbits and roe deer and may be a cheaper alternative to fencing for small areas or where trees are to be planted at wide spacings.

The type of guard commonly available and suitable for forest use is a 1.2 metre high plastic mesh tube 75 mm in diameter, split throughout its length. The guard is wrapped round the tree and the slit edges fastened to each other with metal rings which are provided with the guards. A light stake (e.g. 25 × 25 mm) stapled to the guard is used to keep the guard and plant upright. If only rabbits are present the guards may be halved and used as 0.6 metre high guards. The guards are biodegradable and do not need to be removed, but they need to be inspected to make sure that the leading shoot of the tree is growing vertically inside the guard and has not penetrated the mesh. If the leading shoot has penetrated the mesh, the guard should be slit open, the leading shoot placed inside it, and the slit fastened.

Other larger diameter tree guards are available for use in parkland situations to protect standard trees from deer, sheep and cattle.

Preparing the ground for planting

The work that has to be done before planting trees will depend on whether it is an old woodland site or bare land. The two need different treatments.

Preparing bare ground for planting

The two main jobs to be done in preparing *bare ground* for planting are draining and cultivation.

Draining

Trees will not grow well on waterlogged soil. A high water table results in shallow rooting. Wet soil has little physical strength and trees are more likely to blow down on wet sites. Forest drainage is done by open ditches because tree roots get into pipes and tile drains, and block them. Water does not seem to move sideways in the soil to any noticeable extent, so ditches will not lower the water table, except immediately beside them. To improve conditions for planting on wet sites, furrows are taken out with a draining plough along the planting lines, and the young trees planted on the mound thrown up. It is usual to run the furrows more or less up and down hill so as to avoid getting any flat spots where the water will lie. On sites which are too small to use a plough, turfs can be cut out by hand and inverted, at intervals corresponding to the planting spacing to be used. The young trees are planted on the turfs. An extension of this system is used by the Forestry Commission on heavy, wet soils in South West England. Ditches are taken out with a digger, and bucketfuls of soil are 'dolloped' on either side to provide planting mounds.

In planning a drainage system, first look for water coming on to the site, e.g. from springs, and provide cut-off drains to channel it away. Next plan collecting drains (sometimes called cross-drains) to remove standing water or to catch water running down plough furrows (when they are sometimes called cross-drains). Collecting drains should be spaced, on average, at 40 metres apart but on flatter sites with a slope of less than 3 degrees (1 in 20) the spacing should be reduced to 20 metres. The effective depth of the drain should be about 0.6 metres (2 feet), although where there is a probability of silt collecting, this can be increased to 0.9 metres (3 feet). The slope on the sides of the drain will depend on the shape of the excavator bucket, or the plough being used, but ideally a drain should be about one-third wider at the top than at the bottom. To avoid erosion, the gradient or fall along a drain should not be greater than 2 degrees (1 in 28). When draining valley sides, the drains should slope downwards towards the head of the valley and the gradient on the drain should be eased as it reaches the bottom. To avoid the discharge of silt and debris into the stream (which could cause environmental damage) drains should stop 10-20 metres short of the water-course and the water should be allowed to filter through the streamside vegetation.

Cultivation

In tree-planting, partial cultivation is done for weed-suppression, for local drainage and to provide a surface on which to plant. Complete ploughing is rarely done in forestry. On peaty soils and where local drainage is necessary, shallow furrows are made to give ribbons of turf, about two metres apart, on which the trees are planted. A double-mouldboard plough is often used for this. Where there is a pan in the soil, a tine plough is used to break it up. The use of sub-soiling rippers is coming back into favour for breaking up indurated compacted soils.

Use of herbicides

Extensive experiments have shown that there is strong competition between grass and other ground vegetation and newly planted trees. The practice of cutting the grass or other competing vegetation short may do little or no good at all and can stimulate the grass's requirements for moisture and food. Killing ground vegetation on the planting site by the application of a herbicide in the autumn before spring planting is therefore sound practice. Details of dosages, timing of application and safety measures can be obtained from the firms supplying herbicides and other chemicals for use on the farm.

As an indication of the important role which herbicides can play at the pre-planting stage to provide a clean start for new planting the following general guidance may be useful. A good general herbicide is glyphosate which is foliar-acting, translocating from the treated vegetative growth to the roots, rhizomes or stolons; it becomes rapidly inactive after contact with the soil.

The groups of weeds that may be treated are:

- perennial grasses and grasses mixed with herbaceous broad-leaved weeds;
- woody broadleaved weeds and mixtures of woody and herbaceous broadleaved weeds; and also

- heather;
- rhododendron;
- bracken.

The herbicide should be applied in the summer before planting. Grasses should be treated when they have 10 to 15 cms of actively growing leaf. Woody weeds, heather and bracken are best treated when they are in full leaf or frond but before the foliage changes colour in early autumn. Best results are obtained between mid-July and the end of August.

Rhododendron has a thick waxy leaf and needs high dosages, preferably with an added chemical to help penetration of the leaf.

Early growth of rhododendron can be treated by spraying but older, taller bushes must first be cleared and the stumps treated.

Scrub and unwanted broadleaved species may be too tall to spray effectively, in which case they should be cut first and the exposed stumps treated at once to prevent regrowth and coppicing.

Circular clearing saws can be fitted with an attachment to apply the herbicide directly on to the stump as the stem is being severed. It is useful to add a dye to the herbicide to indicate which stumps have been treated. Best results are obtained in the winter–November to March; do not use this method during the most active period of sap flow in spring and early summer.

Glyphosate controls a wide range of weeds, the main exceptions being gorse and broom. Other herbicides are most specific and may cost less if the range of weeds is more restricted. The principal ones are summarised below.

- Atrazine — soft grasses. Apply early spring.
- Dalapon — grasses. Apply in spring.
- Hexazinone — grasses and some broadleaved weeds. Apply in spring.
- Paraquat — grasses and herbaceous weeds. Weeds with perennial roots are likely to re-grow. Apply in early spring or autumn.
- Propyzamide — grasses and some herbaceous weeds. Apply in winter.
- Asulam — bracken. Apply early summer.
- 2.4-D Ester — heather and broadleaved weeds. Apply early summer.
- Fosamine ammonium — deciduous broadleaved weeds. Apply in summer, weeds die the following year.
- Triclopyr — gorse, broom, rhododendron and a wide range of other weeds except grass and hawthorn.
- Dicamba — bracken control.

Other chemicals may be included in proprietary mixtures with the above.

Reference should be made to *The Code of Practice for the Use of Pesticides in Forestry* which may be obtained from the Forestry Commission.

Old woodland

For one reason or another many farm woodlands have been left unmanaged and are not carrying a full crop of trees. It is impossible to give a general prescription for their rehabilitation. Appearances can be deceptive. For example, a jungle of fallen trees, rotten stems, with a heavy growth of weeds, stool-shoots and suckers may have enough reasonable stems to justify clearing out the rubbish and stocking the gaps in the wood by planting, coppicing or encouraging existing naturally regenerated seedlings. To protect any planted trees or natural regeneration from damage by animals the choice is between making the boundary fence proof against stock, rabbit and possibly deer or using individual tree guards or tree shelters. The choice of planted species may be limited to shade bearers if the gaps between older trees of acceptable form are small and it may be desirable to fell some of them to give more light on the forest floor and so widen the choice to include light-demanding species.

If an old woodland site has recently been felled there may be an accumulation of branchwood. It is advisable to remove larger broadleaved branchwood for firewood and to burn the remainder; usually it is possible to plant through conifer lop and top left after felling, particularly if they are left to decay for a year before planting. On wet sites where ploughing is likely to be difficult and expensive because of old tree stumps and roots, turfs may be dug and placed by hand to provide a raised planting site or advantage may be taken of raised ground near stumps.

It is almost certainly worthwhile to get advice from an experienced forester before carrying out any work on an old neglected woodland. He can often save his fee several times over by specifying the work that needs to be done in that particular wood and pointing out what work need not be undertaken.

3   Planting the trees

Good handling and planting is the *key* to successful survival of
young trees. A well-planted tree, with the roots carefully put in
and firmed down, stands a much better chance of survival. The
amount of beating up of losses depends very much on the
standard of planting.

Planting season

Young trees suffer less if moved when they are dormant, i.e.
when broadleaved trees have lost their leaves and conifers have
hardened-off for the winter. This means that trees can be planted
at any time from late autumn to early spring, depending on the
situation and weather conditions. If conditions are right, late
autumn planting can mean that the trees are able to 'settle-in'
over the winter and make a quick start in the spring, although a
hard frost, soon after planting, can do a lot of damage. The main
planting season is the spring–from late February to early April,
before the trees begin to 'flush'.

   The use of container-grown plants and those which have been
kept in 'cold-store' means that planting of these trees can be done
at almost any time. This may be useful to fit in tree planting with
other farming activities.

Ordering and receiving plants

It is important to order plants in good time from a reputable
forest nurseryman, specifying the size and age of each species.
Generally speaking, on the more exposed sites and on ploughed
ground smaller plants should be used. Where there is heavy
weed-growth and on sheltered sites, larger plants should be used.
(The range of sizes in typical forestry transplants is 20–40 cm.)

The age of transplants is given by showing the number of years in the seedbed plus the number of years in the transplant line– e.g. 1+1, 2+1, 1+2. The longer the period in the transplant line, usually the stronger the plant, but of course it is correspondingly more expensive. In general, small plants suffer less of a shock from planting than large plants, and they are easier to carry and to plant. Herbicides, applied the summer before, give the opportunity to plant on a weed-free site so 20–40 cm plants should be suitable almost everywhere. Larger plants 45–60 cm might be justified in heavy weed growth if herbicides could not be used, or if there is an insoluble rabbit problem. (Rabbits would nibble the side branches of such trees, but would not take out the vital top shoot.) Good plants are sturdy, with a strong stem at the root collar and a good terminal bud. The root system should be well balanced, bushy and compact, and the plants should have been carefully lifted so that the bark of the roots has not been stripped off. On arrival the roots should be moist, and it is important not to let them get dry. The foliage of evergreen conifers should look bright and fresh with no sign of mildew or leaf-fall. Seedlings, other than undercut seedlings which are described later, are not usually as sturdy as transplants, nor do they have such good root systems, and the failure rate is likely to be higher.

Receiving and handling the plants on delivery is very important. Care should be taken to inspect them carefully on arrival and reject any unsuitable ones. If they are not to be planted right away, they should be carefully 'heeled-in' (or 'sheughed' in Scotland), to protect the roots from drying winds or frost. As an emergency measure, the bundles of plants can be piled into 'beehives', with the roots tucked in to protect them. They should not be left for long like this or they may suffer from overheating.

Plastic bags are frequently used to protect plants from drying out after they have been lifted from the nursery. Those coloured black inside and white outside are better than transparent bags as they do not absorb heat to the same degree. Plants will survive in good condition in plastic bags during the cool weather in the early part of the planting season, but if they are received towards the end of the season they should be taken out and heeled in. Plants in bags must be handled and stored carefully. The roots can be damaged if the bags are thrown about or dropped from a height. The bags should be kept upright and left closed, so that water vapour from the plants will condense on the sides and run down to the roots (on the same principle as a bottle garden). They must be kept out of the sun at all times because bright sunshine will quickly raise the temperature enough to kill the plants. Storage on the ground under the canopy of a conifer plantation is ideal, or in a barn. Do not pile the bags on top of one another.

Methods of Planting

Notching

This is the easiest and commonest method of planting young trees (Fig. 3.1). It consists in cutting a slit with a spade, tucking in the roots and firming down. A simple or so-called straight

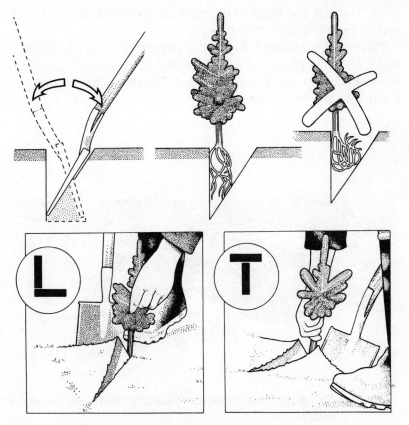

Fig. 3.1 Notch planting with garden spade.

notch is a single slit, cut by one stroke of the spade. This is the easiest and cheapest method, but there is a danger of the plant working its way out again. A better method is with two slits, one at right angles to the other, forming a 'T' or 'L'. The 'flap' made by the two cuts is raised to put in the plant and then tramped down firmly. The young tree is held more securely this way. Variations include 'V' and 'H' notches. On heavy soils always use a notch with more than one slit.

Turfing

Here, the young tree is planted in an over-turned turf. The turf is turned over so that the two layers of grass and vegetation meet and rot away to give added feeding to the young plant. Turfing is suitable on wetter sites, to raise the young plant above the water level. The turf also helps to suppress weeds round the young plant and gives it a chance to get away.

Planting on ploughed ridges is an extension of turfing (Figs. 3.2 and 3.3). If the ploughed ridge is higher than about 22 cm, it may be necessary to cut a 'step', so that the roots can be put more easily into the 'sandwich'.

Fig. 3.2 Ploughing moorland for planting. Furrows 2 metres apart.

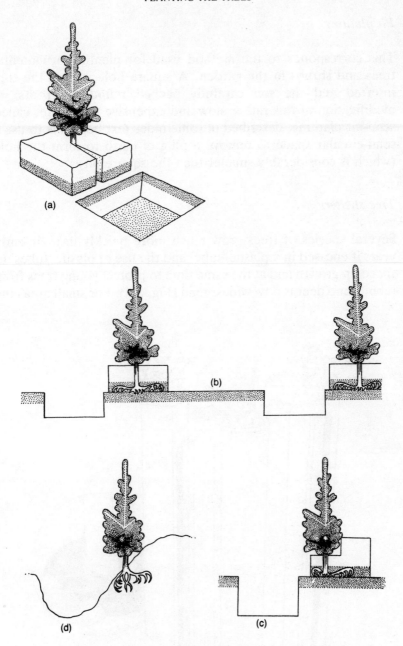

Fig. 3.3 Planting in (a) hand dug turf; (b) ploughed
furrows (2 m apart on peat); (c) step planting on
peat; (d) ploughed mineral soil.

Pit planting

This corresponds to the method used for planting ornamental trees and shrubs in the garden. A square hole is dug, the tree inserted and the soil carefully packed round the roots. A modification of this rather slow and expensive technique, called semi-pit planting, described in some older text books, is to use a semi-circular spade to remove a plug of earth to form the hole (which is considerably smaller than the square pit).

Tree shelters

Several species of trees grow much more quickly in their early years if encased in a plastic 'tube' and the use of plastic 'tubes' to speed up growth and at the same time to protect young trees from rabbits and deer is now widespread (Fig. 3.4). For small areas the

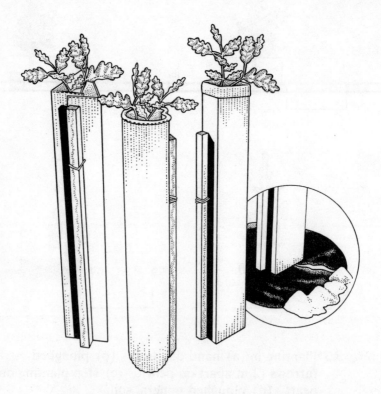

Fig. 3.4 Tree shelters and mulching mat.

overall cost can be less than the cost of traditional planting if the cost of rabbit or deer fencing is taken into account. In other situations it is the greatly enhanced rate of growth in the first few years after planting and easier application of herbicides to suppress ground vegetation that offset the extra initial cost of planting in tree shelters.

A strong stake is driven in near to the planting position and the tree shelter is placed over the plant and firmly fixed to the stake. Tree shelters are useful for promoting the growth of naturally occurring seedlings and protecting them from rabbits and game.

Tree guards fulfil a different function, that of protecting plants against rabbits or deer. They do not enhance growth (Fig. 3.5).

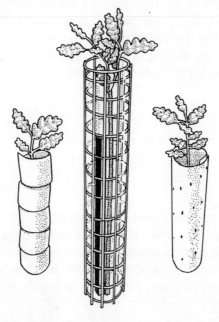

Fig. 3.5 Tree guards–spiral, mesh and sleeve.

The technique of using tree shelters is of relatively recent origin and new types of commercially available shelters continue to appear on the market. Choice is a matter of individual preference, but types in which the wire is placed *round* the outside of the shelter (and therefore also round the tree) may need attention later to remove the wire.

All are made of biodegradable plastic which will rot under the influence of sunlight after a few years.

Several heights are available, the most commonly used being 1.2 metres; in cross section they may be round, square or triangular and are made in a variety of colours.

Tree shelters encourage the growth of weeds within the shelter and do not inhibit weed growth outside it. There are several ways of reducing weed competition. The ground may be treated before planting time with an appropriate weed-killer; if spot application is used an area of at least one metre in diameter should be treated to give adequate protection against weed competition when the tree is planted in the centre of the treated area. A mulching mat may be used or alternatively at planting time a small area may be cleared of weeds with the planting spade before the plant is planted, so that there are no growing weeds inside the tube. Weeds outside the shelter may be treated with herbicide after it is in position at various stages in the growing or dormant season according to the type of chemical used.

Direct-seeding and natural regeneration

Direct-seeding

An alternative to planting-out nursery-grown trees, is to sow the seed directly in the wood. This is not much used in Britain and where it has been tried it has not been very successful. In small areas, with intensive work and attention, it can be done by sowing seed on prepared patches, but is not generally recommended.

Natural regeneration

This is where an existing crop of trees seeds itself. To ensure that an adequate crop of trees results from nature's gift usually requires a careful management. After the initial growth seedlings may die for a variety of reasons and survivors will then perhaps need to be supplemented by beating up. If the regeneration is very prolific and the majority survive then it will need thinning out quite soon. Tree shelters can be used to encourage the growth of selected seedlings where regeneration is sparse to ensure that enough survive to make a crop. Where regeneration is prolific, tree shelters may be placed over a selected few which will soon outgrow the rest and reduce or eliminate the need for early thinning out.

Types of Plants

Seedlings

These are plants raised from seed in a seedbed. Except under very favourable conditions, seedlings are not usually strong enough to survive being planted out and they are usually lifted from the seedbed at the end of their first or second year's growth and planted in another part of the nursery.

Transplants

These are young trees that have been raised in a seedbed and then transplanted to grow on in the nursery for another one or two years. This is the most usual form of plant used in forest planting. The age and size of plant will depend on the site to be planted–the most commonly used being two, three or four year old plants. Their age is described in such a way as to show how long they have spent in the seedbed and how long as transplants in the transplant lines, e.g. 1+1 = 1 year in seedbed and 1 year in transplant lines; 1+2 = 1 year in seedbed and 2 years in transplant lines.

Undercutting

To give a bushy fibrous root system, seedlings or transplants may have their roots cut off a few cms below ground level using a tractor-drawn knife. The cutting is timed during the growing season to ensure that there is adequate time for new rootlets to grow before the end of the growing season. The letter U in a catalogue of seedlings or transplants indicates that they have been undercut.

Whips

These are 65–170 cm high broadleaved trees. They have the advantage of being able to compete with ground vegetation better than smaller transplants but they can suffer from drying out and may need watering in dry weather. They are vulnerable to damage by stock and animals and may need protection. They are much more expensive than transplants.

Standards

These are trees over 2 metres in height. They are very expensive, need careful planting and have a lower survival rate and are not generally used in woodland planting.

Spacing

Transplants

The normal spacing for planting out transplants when planting up bare land is about 2 m apart, to give about 2500 plants per ha (or 1000 per acre). On old woodland sites wider spacings in a matrix of regrowth may be used, especially in broadleaved woodland.

Whips and standards

These are planted much wider apart–at least three metres, which means about 1100 per ha.

Tools and equipment

Garden spade

This is the simplest, best and most commonly used tool for tree-planting. A well-worn spade with sharpened blade, gives a clean cut and can be used for all types of planting. Some specialised variants have been made but an ordinary garden spade takes a lot of beating (Fig. 3.6).

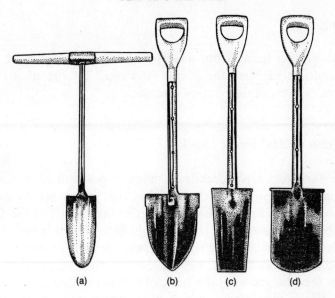

Fig. 3.6 Planting spades.   (a) Semicircular–for planting in
turves, mounds or peat;   (b) Schlich–for planting in
hard or stony ground;   (c) Mansfield–for planting in
hard ground or peat;   (d) Garden–for most general
planting.

Mattock

This tool, with a blade on one side and a pick on the other, is
useful for planting on steep banks and rocky sites. It can be used
in a crouching or kneeling position where it is difficult to work
standing upright. It can be used for screefing, notching, and even
for mounding or pit-planting.

Semi-circular spade

This is a specialised spade consisting of a semi-circular tube with a
handle at right angles to the vertical shaft. It is used to take out a
cylindrical core of soil or peat, the roots of the plant are pushed
into the hole and the plug replaced. It really needs a two-man team
to use, one to make the holes and the other to plant the trees.

Planting bag

A planting bag made from waterproof material and hung from the shoulders to carry the plants–and most important, to keep their roots from drying out–is essential.

Protection against insect attack

Where a conifer crop succeeds a conifer crop within a few years of it being felled there is a danger that the young plants will be attacked by the Large pine weevil (*Hylobius abietis*) or the Black pine beetle (*Hylastes* spp.). The Large pine weevil breeds in the stumps and roots of conifers. The grubs live in burrows beneath the bark and emerge as weevils one or two years later. The weevils feed by gnawing the bark of newly planted conifers.

The Black pine beetle which also breeds in conifer stumps feeds below the bark of young conifers near ground level and may cause death by girdling the tree.

Protection is by dipping the whole plant in a water-suspension of gamma HCH if the Large pine weevil and the Black pine beetle are both present on the felled conifer site. If the Large pine weevil only is present, only the aerial part of the plant needs to be dipped.

Other weevils that can cause damage to young conifers include the Small brown weevil, (*Strophosomus melongrammus*) and the Clay-coloured weevil (*Otiorrhynchus singularis*). Control is by spraying with gamma HCH.

For all operations involving chemicals appropriate protective clothing must be worn. Get advice from the chemical manufacturer through your normal chemical supplier. Alternatively it may be worth using the services of an established contracting firm with knowledge and experience in the techniques of dipping, handling and planting in infested areas.

4 Caring for Young Trees

There is a temptation to feel that once the trees have been planted there is nothing else to be done for a long time. But unless the young trees are carefully looked after, all the money and effort that has gone into preparing the ground and planting them will be wasted. The most important continuing task is to keep down competition from other vegetation, i.e. by weeding. Less important usually is the replacement of trees that have died– called 'beating up'.

Beating Up

Very seldom, if ever, can one expect 100 per cent survival of newly-planted trees. Losses of up to about 10 per cent can be accepted. Beating up must be done where overall losses are greater than this, or where entire patches have failed.

While beating up should not be delayed too long, wait until the end of the first growing season before assessing the losses. If summer weeding is carried out some first idea of the extent of losses may be obtained. A full assessment can be made later, in the autumn, and replacement plants ordered for the coming planting season.

Larger plants are sometimes used for beating up, to give them a greater chance to catch up with the original planting. Unless it was obviously a wrong choice in the first place, beating up is usually done with the same species. If repeated beating up is needed over a number of years, then the later beating up can be done with a quicker growing species.

Weeding

Many kinds of vegetation compete with young trees, including grasses, heather, bracken, bramble and rushes. A thick mat of grass can choke a young tree and compete for moisture; heather can inhibit the growth of spruces by more effectively competing for nitrogen in the soil; dead bracken can damage young trees when it falls in the autumn, especially if later covered by snow; brambles and honeysuckle can strangle young trees.

It was at one time standard practice to cut back all vegetation that was competing for nutrients, moisture and space or which would smother the young trees in autumn when it dried and collapsed. However, over-weeding can sometimes do more harm than not weeding. In a dry season the shade of a cover of bracken or other weeds can even be beneficial, and recent research by the Forestry Commission has shown that the regrowth of cut-over weeds can be so vigorous as to require more moisture than the original weeds. Where weeding is desirable, the solution often is to use a herbicide.

Methods of Weeding

Hand-weeding

A grass-hook or sickle was for many years the only tool used for weeding in young woods. It is still used in small areas and where other methods are not possible. It is labour-intensive and needs skilled and experienced persons to do it. Care has to be taken to avoid cutting the young trees ('Sheffield blight').

Mechanical weeding

On larger areas of trees, where they were planted sufficiently wide apart, machines such as autoscythes and gang-mowers were used. The result looked very good but was often quite ineffective in reducing competition, and as mentioned above might be harmful on dry sites in dry seasons.

Chemical weeding

Herbicides can be used for weeding provided precautions are taken to avoid damage to crop trees.

Broadleaved trees are likely to be damaged or killed by herbicide spray or drift while they are in leaf and so weeds in broadleaved plantations can only be treated with a guarded sprayer (Fig. 4.1) or with granular herbicides applied in winter. A placed application can be made by using a rope wick applicator (commonly called a weed wiper). Conifers, except larch, are more resistant, and some species can be treated with overall sprays at the end of the growing season, when the buds at the ends of the shoots have hardened off. The date of hardening off varies with different species (pines being earliest), and to some extent with the season. It can be as early as July or as late as October. Some tree species have a second period of growth (Lammas growth) in late summer. The time of hardening off can only be determined by inspecting the plantation. As most herbicides need to be applied before the weeds start to die back, usually in late September, chemical weeding is concentrated in a short period in late summer. If the leaves of weed species have started to change colour it is too late for an effective kill. If it is

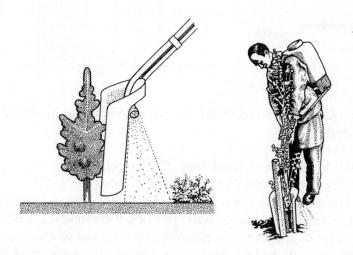

Fig. 4.1 Applying herbicide with Arbogard to protect tree.

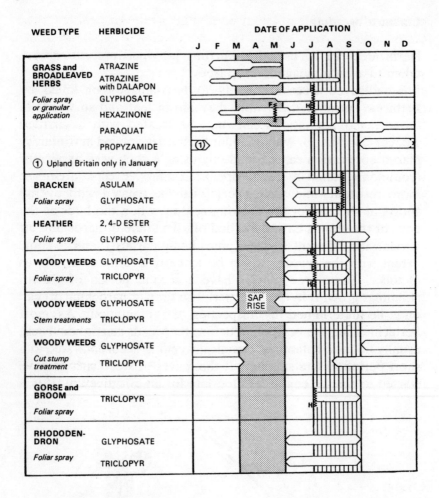

Fig. 4.2 Adapted from the Forestry Commission Herbicide Chart.

F=Flushing period.

H=Earliest date of hardening-off of crop.

S=Commencement of senescence of weeds.

The information in this chart is of a very general nature and is for illustrative guidance only; individual seasons may show divergence from these limits. Details essential to effective treatment are to be found in the appropriate sections of F.C. Booklet 51 *The Use of Herbicides in the Forest* currently being revised.

necessary to apply herbicides in conifer plantations earlier, this can be done by using a guard or a placed spray to avoid the crop.

Species vary in their susceptibility to different herbicides. Sitka spruce, Norway spruce, Scots pine, Corsican pine, lodgepole pine, western red cedar and Lawson's cypress, are tolerant to glyphosate provided the buds have hardened. Douglas fir is rather more sensitive. Glyphosate should not be applied when rain is expected as it takes up to 24 hours to be sufficiently absorbed by the foliage. If used later than June it will not significantly reduce the weed competition in the current season. Christmas trees and ornamental species should not be sprayed as their appearance may be affected by even slight spray damage.

Details of crop sensitivity to other herbicides were given in the Forestry Commission Booklet 51, *The Use of Herbicides in the Forest*, which was until recently obtainable from the Forest Research Station, Alice Holt Lodge, Wrecclesham, Farnham, Surrey, and in other Forestry Commission publications. This booklet will be revised and reprinted by the beginning of 1989. Until the new edition is available enquiries will be dealt with by correspondence. Many herbicide manufacturers also provide helpful booklets and information sheets. The use of herbicides is now governed by the Control of Pesticides Regulations 1986. Pesticides should always be used in accordance with recommended rates and precautions and appropriate protective clothing should be worn.

Cleaning

'Cleaning takes place just before canopy closure. It involves cutting or killing herbaceous plants, woody plants such as shrubs, broadleaved regrowth from stool-shoots, brambles and climbers such as honeysuckle. These may be cut back by hand tools or mechanical hand-held brush-cutter; but with great care it is possible to use a 'brushkiller' chemical. Larger stems of such regrowth can be girdled or frayed and painted with chemical. Specialist advice should be sought from forestry consultants, the Forestry Commission or the manufacturers before using chemicals.

Maintenance of drains and fences

Drains

These should be kept free-running and cleared out when necessary. In small areas, this is probably best done by hand with a shovel. In more extensive areas it can be done by machine.

Fences

So long as young crops are vulnerable, it is important to keep the fences secure against farmstock and other animals. Regular inspection and repair is vital. It may not be necessary to keep up rabbit netting after the trees are out of danger, but deer fencing may have to be maintained for a much longer period.

Establishment

When the crop is fully-stocked, growing well and free of competition, it is considered to be established. By then or soon after the canopy will have closed, the branches of adjacent trees will be touching and little or no light will reach the ground, and weeds and competing vegetation will mostly have been suppressed. It will then be safe to leave the young trees alone until the thinning stage is reached. Thinning is often preceded by brashing (i.e. the removal of the lower branches) to ease access for inspection and marking the trees to be removed, and for access for shooting. Brashing and thinning are discussed in Chapters 6 and 7.

5 Damage to Woodlands

Trees and woodlands can suffer damage in a number of ways. They can be damaged by wind, frost, or fire. They can suffer from pests and diseases and be attacked by animals and birds. But apart from occasional extensive windthrow caused by gales of exceptional severity, the majority of woodlands, given proper management, will survive to maturity.

Wind

Shallow-rooting species–such as spruce–are liable to windthrow on most sites but deeper rooting species (like the larches and Douglas fir) are also liable to windthrow on shallow soils or soils with impeded drainage, especially on exposed ground. Thinning that has been delayed brings extra risk of windthrow. Windthrow varies from the risk of a few scattered trees in winter gales to the opening up of small gaps in the canopy which may enlarge over time. Windthrow is often associated with the thinning of a stand. Thin early and often rather than late and at long intervals is the time-honoured dictum for all situations where there is a risk of windthrow. If thinning in high-risk areas has been long delayed it may be advisable to go for a policy of no thinning and accept a shorter rotation. In some sites of very high windthrow risk it may be wise to adopt a 'no thin' policy from the outset.

Frost

Young trees can suffer from frost–particularly in late spring after they have started growing. One of the best safeguards is to avoid 'frost-hollows' for planting. Where they exist, care can be taken to make sure that the cold air can flow out and is not dammed by a belt of trees or other obstruction. Some trees are more resistant to frost than others–for example, Norway spruce is more tolerant than Sitka spruce–so choice of species is important if planting up frosty sites. Scots pine and Norway maple are frost-resistant.

Fire

Forest fires in Britain seldom start by natural causes such as lightning. They are usually the result of human carelessness, e.g. heather, grass or stubble burning, which gets out of hand. The local fire brigades have a duty to attend any uncontrolled fire and their fire prevention officers are always willing to discuss safety measures. It is worth asking for a visit.

Damage by animals and birds

Farm livestock

Sheep, cattle, horses, pigs and goats can all do serious damage to trees. Sheep and goats can browse young tree-shoots, especially in winter if there is no bite of grass. Horses can strip the bark of older trees and if they completely ring the stem can kill them. Cattle are more likely to churn up ('poach') the ground and interfere with the drainage and damage the tree roots. In the uplands where snow storms are a regular occurrence quite small areas in woodland can be fenced off as emergency cattle winter feeding areas in times of snow storm. To be of any use they must be adjacent to fields where the cattle graze and accessible by tractor and trailer so that regular and adequate supplies of hay or other food can be brought to the wood. While it is possible to allow grazing in woodland, it *must* be properly controlled. Otherwise, the best thing is to keep farm livestock out of the woods with adequate fencing.

Wild animals

Rabbits and hares can do a lot of damage to newly planted trees and young natural regrowth. Deer–roe, red, fallow, sika and muntjac–are all present in different parts of the country. They can do damage by browsing and fraying with their antlers. Control measures include deer-fencing and keeping the populations within reasonable numbers by shooting. Safe and humane methods must be used. (Consult the Game Conservancy or the Forestry Commission for further information.)

The native red squirrel does damage to conifer plantations in some parts of Scotland but control measures are seldom required. The introduced grey squirrel, on the other hand, is a major pest of broadleaved woodlands and must be controlled. It causes damage by stripping bark from the stem and branches during the months of May-July. As a result the crowns may be deformed, or the top of the tree may die. Damage is also done to the trunk at ground level. Most tree species, even conifers, are at risk, but sycamore and beech in the pole stage are most susceptible. Since squirrels migrate readily, control should be carried out in susceptible crops during April-July only. The most effective method is to use a warfarin bait, in specially designed hoppers to reduce the risk to other wildlife. This use is defined in the Grey Squirrels (Warfarin) Order 1973 and warfarin may not be used in certain designated counties (in effect, those where the red squirrel is still present). The alternative is to use cage traps. Forestry Commission leaflet 56, *Grey Squirrel Control*, gives fuller information.

The 1981 Wildlife and Countryside Act provides the most comprehensive guidance to legislation on shooting, trapping and poisoning wild animals.

Birds

On the whole, these do not damage trees although grouse, blackgame and capercaillie can eat young shoots and buds. A colony of starlings can damage established woods by the concentration of their droppings poisoning the soil.

Pests and diseases

Damage can be caused to trees by insects, fungi, bacteria and viruses, but the first two are the most important. The main defence against diseases is to choose species that will thrive as opposed to those that will do less well on the site. The following notes refer to the most commonly encountered pests and diseases.

Insects

Insects attack tree seed and seedlings and transplants in nurseries. Insects attacking young trees in woodlands include the Large pine weevil and Black pine beetles which attack newly planted conifers on conifer sites that have been restocked shortly after the old crop has been felled. Two other weevils that attack forest trees, are the clay-coloured weevil (*Otiorrhynchus*) and a small brown weevil (*Stropohosomus melanogrammus*). Control is discussed in Chapter 3.

In the first ten years or so after establishment, sap sucking adelgids may be conspicuous on conifers such as Douglas fir, the larches and the spruces, and pine sawflies on the pines. In crops of young broadleaves defoliation may also occur. Generally it is neither economic nor essential for the life of the crop to try to control these insects and most conifers and broadleaves survive.

In older woods defoliators are mostly the caterpillars of moths and sawflies, although aphids are responsible for the defoliation of some species–Sitka spruce, for example. Some defoliators are well known, such as the Oak Leaf Roller moth which periodically damages older oak woods; others are known only in some regions like the Pine Beauty moth which has attacked lodgepole pine in North Scotland. If widespread defoliation is evident it is essential to get professional advice. The Forestry Commission is the body to contact.

The principal insect pests of economic importance are summarised below:

Pine weevil–infests the stumps and roots of felled conifers. The adult gnaws the bark of young conifer trees. Control by the use of an approved insecticide–seek Forestry Commission guidance.

Black pine beetle–breeds in stumps and roots of felled conifer trees. The adult gnaws the bark of the roots of young conifer trees. Control as for pine weevil.

Pine shoot beetle–adult beetle bores up the centre of Scots pine

twigs which then fall off. The crowns look thin and broken shoots
with hollow centres are found on the ground. The beetle breeds
under the bark of fresh logs or moribund trees which look as if
they have been peppered with shot after the beetles have
emerged. Control is by removing felled trees and logs promptly
(within 6 weeks) during the breeding season, March-July.

Pine looper moth–eats the needles of pines and completely
defoliates the tree, young and old shoots alike. Control by aerial
spraying but consult the Forestry Commission first.

Pine beauty moth–a pest of lodgepole pine in Scotland. It attacks
developing needles of the new shoots in spring and moves onto
the older needles later. Control by aerial spraying but consult the
Forestry Commission.

Pine sawfly–sawfly caterpillars differ from those of butterflies
and moths by having a pair of legs on each segment of their
bodies. The caterpillars eat the needles of pines but leave the
current year's growth. Yellow pupae are found on the twigs.
Biological control is possible, using a virus. Get advice from the
Forestry Commission.

Spruce sawfly–eats the needles of Sitka and Norway spruce.
Control as for Pine sawfly.

Felted beech coccus–a small sucking insect which attacks the bark
of beech trees and covers itself with a waxy, woolly secretion.
Severe infestation weakens the tree and allows the entry of beech
bark disease (see Fungi, below). No control is practicable but
crop vigour should be promoted by thinning.

Spruce bark beetle (*Dendroctonus*)–discovered in Britain in 1980s
and at present confined to Wales and the West of England where
there are strict control regulations. It lays eggs under the bark of
spruces, and the larvae, advancing *en masse*, kill large patches of
bark and may kill the tree. In the early stages, infestation may be
detected by the entry points of the adults, known as resin tubes.
These are made of resin mixed with chewed bark, and are rather
like small worm casts, with a hole in the middle. They are often
associated with old wounds on the tree. In the active season in
mid-summer, chewed bark or 'frass' looking like fine sawdust may
be noticed at the foot of the tree. Control is by strict hygiene–felling
and debarking. Report to the Forestry Commission. A predator
beetle, Rhizophagus, has been released and may achieve a
natural control.

Fungi

These, too, can attack trees in various ways. There are root-rots, butt-rots, die-back and canker. Obvious signs of attack are bracket-like growths on the stem or groups of toadstools appearing on the ground nearby. The fungal growth may also be hidden under the bark or wrapped round the roots. The commonest fungus attacking conifers in Britain is the Fomes Root-rot which attacks through the roots; that attacking the roots of both conifers and broadleaves is the Honey fungus. Fomes is present in most areas that have previously carried coniferous crops. The development of the disease can be retarded by treating freshly cut stumps at the time of felling or thinning with a solution of urea or in the case of pines with the spores of another fungus that prevents the invasion by Fomes.

Of importance in beech is beech bark disease. The bark is first infested by the felted beech coccus which allows entry of the fungus (*Nectria*). The disease appears as a black spot on the bark 1–2 cm in diameter which oozes black slime. The cankers increase in size and large areas of bark die, eventually killing the tree. Infected trees can sometimes be detected by smaller leaves and early yellowing of foliage. Prompt felling of infected trees is necessary if the timber is to be utilised.

The most important bacterial disease is that attacking poplars with the formation of black cankers, and the tree may be killed. A white slime oozes from splits in the bark of twigs, branches or young stems in spring. Extensive die back is likely to occur. A list of disease-resistant varieties of poplar may be obtained from the Forestry Commission, and only these should be planted.

As with serious insect pest attacks, the Forestry Commission is the authority to contact if there are obvious signs of disease on trees or if there are unexplained deaths in the crop.

6 Brashing and Pruning

'Brashing' is the removal of the lower branches in a conifer crop, after the canopy has closed, to a height of about 2 metres to give sufficient headroom for easy access through the wood (Fig. 6.1). Anyone who has tried to get through an unbrashed Sitka spruce plantation to inspect it will appreciate the advantage of brashing. In a brashed plantation it is relatively easy to see if anything has gone wrong–for example, sporadic windthrow.

Fig. 6.1 Brashing to 2 m height.

Where pheasant shooting is important, complete brashing is done to allow the beaters to get through and to help hold the birds in the brash. Also, where amenity or public access is important complete brashing may be done. For ordinary purposes of forest management, complete brashing is not necessary and a smaller number of trees may be brashed either in rows or selectively throughout the crop to give access for inspection and marking trees for thinning. This is obviously a lot cheaper than complete brashing.

Brashing is best done by hand with a sharp curved pruning saw. Brashing by chain-saw requires great skill and is not recommended for general use. It is essential that a clean cut is made close to the stem. With a sharp saw the smaller branches can be cut off with a single pulling stroke of the saw. The branches of larch can sometimes be knocked off with a stick.

Brashing is labour-intensive but since it is something that can be done when other work is not possible in winter, it can fit in well with farm work.

Brashing can be thought of as a preliminary to marking the trees to come out in the first thinning, which is discussed in the next chapter.

High pruning

High pruning is done to improve the quality of the timber by removing branches. It is done to a greater height than brashing so as to give a butt-length of saw timber free of knots of at least four metres on selected trees of good form and vigour. Pruning must be done early in the life of a tree when the stem diameter at the point where it is being pruned is not more than 15 cms. Cutting away too much of the green crown of the tree can slow down growth, so pruning is usually done in a number of lifts until the desired pruning height is reached (Fig. 6.2). Long handled pruning saws are needed; the alternative is to use a ladder.

The branch should be cut off to leave the branch collar (Fig. 6.3) which will quickly grow over the exposed area. If the branch is cut off too close to the stem, healing takes longer.

Pruning is only worth doing if it makes a real contribution to improving the timber quality of final crop trees. It is arguable whether the timber merchant will pay a sufficiently large premium for pruned trees to cover the cost to the grower of the pruning operations. On the other hand, if pruning is carried out at times when there is little alternative work on the farm the real cost to the farmer may be quite small, and the trees will certainly be more saleable provided that proper records are kept showing the ages and sizes of tree when successive pruning operations were undertaken.

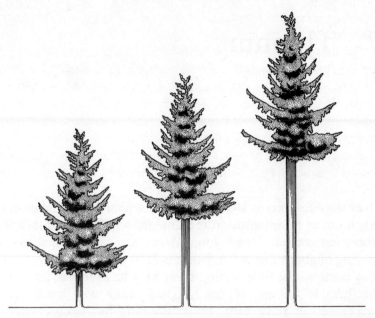

Fig. 6.2 Pruning in 3 stages of 2 m each.

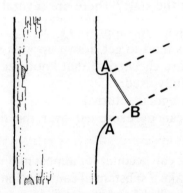

Fig. 6.3 Pruning cut branch at A–A to leave branch collar–
not at A–B.

7 Thinning

Over the life-time of a crop, as great a volume of timber can be taken out in thinnings as in the final felling. When establishing a woodland on bare land young trees are usually planted at a spacing of about 2 m × 2 m which is 2500 per hectare. By the time they come to the final felling, there may be as few as 200 trees to the hectare. Some of the original trees will have become suppressed or have died, but if thinning has been carried out regularly the bulk of them will have been harvested and utilised.

If only 200 trees per hectare are needed for the final crop, why plant so many at the start? There are several reasons:

- close spacing helps to suppress weeds;
- the young trees tend to get drawn up with straight stems;
- side branches are checked so that knot size is reduced;
- the ground is fully used;
- thinnings give regular returns;
- more control can be exercised over the development of the crop.

Since thinnings can account for almost half the total yield of the crop, they can make a substantial contribution to the total income earned from a woodland and can provide a welcome positive cash flow long before the crop is mature and due for its final felling. Early thinnings, which comprise trees of small size, are relatively expensive to harvest and tend to attract prices at the lower end of the market. But when demand for wood is strong, even early thinnings will show a surplus (the difference between the price obtained and the cost of harvesting and transporting to the point of sale).

As to demand for roundwood, the situation in Britain is that in the past few years there has been a massive investment in a whole range of new wood processing plants employing the very latest technologies, so that almost everywhere roundwood of all kinds, including thinnings, is eagerly sought after. The prospects for future expansion are good, not least because the existing British wood processing industry can only meet about an eighth of demand.

In coniferous woodlands early thinnings provide much of the raw material for the paper-pulp industries and to a lesser extent of the various building board and chipboard industries (some of which are based on wood residues). Round fencing absorbs large quantities of conifer thinnings. By middle age, there is a substantial yield of small-sized sawlogs. Thinnings from broad-leaved woodlands are used–to a more limited extent than conifers–for making paper-pulp, fibreboard and chipboard. They have specialised local uses such as turnery poles, cleft oak posts and cleft ash fencing rails, sawn hardwood mining timber, and as firewood for domestic wood-burning stoves.

When to thin

The age at which the first thinning is carried out will depend on the rate of height growth of the trees. Trees planted at a normal spacing will be ready for a first thinning when they reach about 8–10 metres in height. This can be as early as 15 years on good sites for really fast-growing trees, such as grand fir, Douglas fir or Japanese larch, but may be up to 30 years for slower-growing trees like oak or Scots pine. Forestry Commission Booklet 54, *Thinning Control* gives a table for thinning ages of various species and yield classes.

Which trees to remove

There are two different ways of carrying out a thinning. It can be done in a completely automatic way, e.g. by taking out every third, fourth or fifth tree or every third, fourth or fifth row of trees. This is called mechanical or non-selective thinning. The other method is called selective thinning because the trees to be removed are selected individually.

Selective thinning improves the crop by getting rid of the poorer quality trees. After a mechanical thinning you are likely still to have the same proportion of bad trees as you had before, but the vigour and rate of growth of the trees that remain will be much improved. A compromise often adopted is to thin mechanically by removing rows of trees (so-called line thinning) for the first thinning and then thinning selectively thereafter.

The choice of trees to be removed in a selective thinning is made easier if the trees in a stand are thought of as falling into one of seven categories (Fig. 7.1):

Fig. 7.1 Classification of trees: (a) suppressed; (b) whip;
(c) sub-dominant; (d) co-dominant; (e) dominant;
(f) dead or dying; (g) wolf.

(1) Dominant trees – these are the tallest and biggest trees in the stand.
(2) Co-dominants – these are smaller than dominant trees; they are a substantial component of the stand.
(3) Sub-dominants – definitely and obviously smaller than co-dominants.

(4) Suppressed   – likely to die in time.

(5) Dead or dying.

(6) Wolf   – a dominant or co-dominant that is rough, heavily branched and of poor stem form.

(7) Whip   – a dominant, co-dominant or sub-dominant that has a narrow crown and a thin stem; such trees are flexible and liable to 'whip' in strong winds.

Remembering that the object of thinning is to benefit the growth of the trees remaining after thinning and to improve the overall quality of the stand in terms of tree shape, a first priority of every selective thinning is to remove wolf trees and whips and to reduce competition for crown space by thinning out the dominants and co-dominants. Usually it makes little difference to the growth rate of the dominants if the suppressed trees are left; they may well die by the time of the next thinning and some prefer to remove them whilst they are alive and utilisable. This leaves the question of the sub-dominants. Their influence on the rate of growth of the best of the dominants will not be very great and they may help to reduce the growth of branches of dominants and sub-dominants by shading the crowns from light.

A not uncommon fault in thinning is to concentrate too much on the removal of sub-dominants, suppressed, dying and dead trees, believing that what will undoubtedly be a much tidier looking stand has been thinned. Thinning always implies the removal of some dominants and co-dominants.

What of existing woodlands that have not been regularly thinned in the past and are over-stocked? The answer must be to proceed with caution, especially on exposed sites and on shallow or poorly drained soils. If in doubt seek professional advice; it may be prudent to adopt a no-thin regime to reduce the risk of windthrow.

At the other end of the scale there may be woodlands that are under-stocked, where no thinning is required. Table 7.1 gives some help in deciding if a woodland is under- or over-stocked.

The relationship between tree size and age of tree is of the order given in Table 7.2.

These figures are based on the average tree diameter in woodlands growing on Grade 4 land (MAFF classification); within the woodland there will be a considerable range of individual tree sizes round the average.

Table 7.1

	Average tree diameter at breast height (cm)					
	10–20	20–30	30–40	40–50	50–60	over 65
Overstocked if:						
spacing less than (metres)	2	3	4	5	7	8
trees more than (number per ha)	2000	800	600	400	200	150
Normal if:						
spacing (metres)	2.5–3.5	4–6	5–7	6–8	8–10	10–14
trees (number per ha)	800–1700	300–600	200–400	150–300	100–150	50–100
Understocked if:						
spacing more than (metres)	4	7	9	10	12	16
trees less than (number per ha)	600	200	150	100	70	40

Table 7.2

	Diameter at breast height in cm:				
	10	20	30	40	50
	Age in years				
Beech	35	55	75	95	115
Oak	30	50	70	90	120
Ash, cherry, sycamore, walnut	20	30	40	60	
Alder, birch	15	25	35		
Larch	15	30	45	70	
Pine	20	40	60	80	
Spruce	25	40	55	80	

Source: ADAS–*Practical Work in Farm Woods.*

The only accurate way of deciding whether a wood is over- or under-stocked is by assessing the basal area (see Appendix 3– Measuring Timber). The 'threshold' basal area (i.e. the basal area at which the stand is considered fully stocked and ready for thinning) depends on the species and on the height. Forestry Commission Booklet 54, *Thinning Control*, gives a table of threshold basal areas, and should be consulted before thinning is undertaken. Over-thinning can lead to loss of production because the site is under-used, as well as making the crop liable to windthrow.

Marking and thinning

There are two ways of approaching the choice of trees to be removed in a selective thinning. The first is to mark (say with paint) the best trees that are to stay on to form final-crop trees and then come back a second time to mark (say, with a blaze) those trees around them that are to be removed–which will always include those that are judged to be interfering with their growth. This is a fairly time-consuming process but is probably worthwhile in crops that have already been thinned several times. For first and second thinnings it is enough to walk through the stand and mark those trees that are to be removed; of course, the mental process is much the same as one is constantly identifying good trees and thinning round them to give them more room to grow.

In mechanical thinning there is, strictly speaking, no need to mark the trees to come out. Fellers can be told to remove every xth tree in every yth row. But if thinnings are to be cut by contractors then it may be desirable to mark the trees to be cut to avoid any possible misunderstandings.

Respacing or non-commercial thinning

Sometimes, when trees have been planted at normal spacing but thinning would be uneconomic, a very early thinning can be carried out even before the canopy closes. In this case, the cut trees are just left lying on the forest-floor to rot away. Subsequent thinnings can be carried out in the normal way.

No-thin regime

It is possible to calculate with some precision where the risks of windthrow following thinning are so high that it is better to leave the crop unthinned throughout its lifetime. The Forestry Commission or a forestry consultant can give this information for individual sites.

8   Felling the Final Crop

When to fell the final crop?

There are several factors which should be taken into consideration when deciding on the age at which a tree crop should be felled. Similar factors influence the decision as to when felling should begin and how quickly it should proceed if the crop is to be replaced gradually over a period of time by the felling of groups.

The factors include:

- rate of growth of the crop;
- risk of windblow;
- prices of timber;
- the owner's financial situation;
- amenity, nature conservation and sporting interests.

Rotation age as a function of rate of growth

Trees start to grow slowly, then as the canopy closes there is a period of vigorous growth which eventually terminates in a period of no growth. If left long enough the stand may then show negative growth as old trees die. A typical growth curve is shown in Fig. 8.1. The *current annual* increase in volume rises rapidly and peaks at about 35 years of age. The *mean annual* increment rises more slowly and reaches a maximum at around 55 years, at point R. This indicates that the age at which the crop should be felled (rotation age) is around 55 years to obtain the maximum profit from the crop. As mentioned below, rotation age is only one of the factors which will influence an individual owner's decision as to when to fell a crop, but it is a key factor that should alert the owner to the need to consider felling the crop.

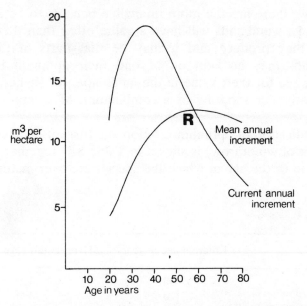

Fig. 8.1 A typical growth curve for Sitka spruce of average
rate of growth. Rotation age is about 55 years, when
the mean annual increment is a maximum.

In Britain the risk of windthrow increases with the height of the
trees and on sites of high risk from windthrow there will be a
maximum height at which it is prudent to fell if the near certainty
of windthrow is to be averted. It is necessary to get professional
advice on the critical height at which to fell.

Generally speaking, price per unit volume increases with
increasing tree size until a point is reached when further increase
in tree size brings little or no price benefit and in some situations
may even bring a penalty. Broadly speaking the price-size curve is
similar to the rate of growth curve and the financial rotation age is
similar to the rotation age based on growth rates. There are a few
exceptions such as transmission poles where small increases in
diameter at breast height can bring large increases in price.

Rotation age is a flexible concept and as the wood and wood
products market is cyclical an owner may feel he is able to wait a
few years or fell a little prematurely to take advantage of high
demand and good prices. Again, the owner's own financial
position–e.g. his need to raise capital in a particular year–may
override other considerations.

Finally, there are the more intangible benefits to be assessed since most woodlands will have a value other than that of the timber they produce and it may be that parts of the farm woodlands may be kept on beyond their optimum financial rotation age for their value in the landscape, for shelter, nature conservation or shooting or a combination of several of these factors.

An indication of optimum rotation age (except on sites with a high risk of windthrow) is shown in Table 8.1, together with an indication of the age at which the species are over-mature.

Table 8.1

	Rotation age in years	Over-mature–age in years
Ash	90	120
Beech	120	180
Birch	50	60
Cherry	70	80
Oak	150	250
Sweet chestnut	90	200
Sycamore	75	200
Larch	50	100
Pine	60/70	100
Spruce	50/60	100

It will be seen that oak, sweet chestnut and sycamore offer great flexibility in the choice of age of felling. Unless special markets are known to exist for older trees, it is probably better not to retain conifers more than 20 years beyond their rotation age.

9 Harvesting the Trees

Felling trees is a dangerous occupation. The larger the tree the greater the risks. A mature tree will weigh up to 3 or 4 tonnes and the force that it exerts as it falls will be much greater, especially if there is a wind blowing.

The chain-saw is used almost exclusively to-day for felling and trimming the branches (Fig. 9.1). It is a dangerous tool. Chain-saw accidents are seldom trivial and can result in the loss of an arm or a leg or in death. *A chain-saw should only be used after proper basic training by a skilled instructor and then only by operators wearing the appropriate protective helmet, ear-muffs, vizor and clothing* (Fig. 9.2). A modern saw should be used since it will incorporate safety features lacking on earlier saws; the right choice of saw from a specialist dealer will help to reduce accidents.

A Throttle lock out
B ON/OFF switch
C Combined chain brake, front hand guard
D Deadhand safety throttle
E Chain breakage guard
F Anti–vibration system
G Chain Catcher
H Safety chain

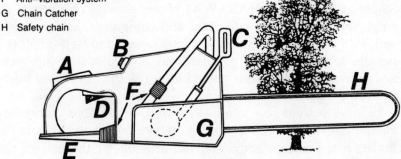

Fig. 9.1 Power saw or chain-saw.

A   Safety helmet, ear defenders,
    eye protection
B   Close-fitting jacket

C   Gloves with protective pad on
    the back of the left hand
D   Protective trousers

E   Chain saw operator's boots

Fig. 9.2 Chain-saw operator's protective clothing.

The criteria which chain-saws must meet are laid down in The Agriculture (Field Machinery) Regulations. The 1974 Health and Safety at Work Act (HASAWA) places general obligations on employers to maintain safe plant and equipment, safe premises and safe systems of work; on employees and self-employed persons to work in a safe manner; and on employers, employees and self-employed persons not to put at risk the health and safety of third parties.

Helpful leaflets on chain-saws and other tree harvesting equipment and advice on training courses are available from the bodies listed under 'additional information' at the end of this chapter.

In view of the greater risks in the harvesting of large trees, the felling of mature and large trees should be left to skilled professionals. However, many farmers may feel that they are capable of harvesting early thinnings and other small to medium-sized trees. The basic techniques are described below.

Felling

Before starting to fell any tree regardless of its size care must be taken to ensure that a clear escape route has been prepared so that the feller can get out of the way rapidly should the tree start to fall in the wrong direction.

To fell a tree, first cut a V-shaped notch at the base of the stem on that side of the tree on which it is desired that it should fall (Fig. 9.3). This cut–the *sink*–may be made by chain-saw or axe. The top cut is made first. Top and bottom cut should meet exactly–at a depth of about one quarter of the diameter of the butt of the tree. Then make the *felling cut* from the other side of the tree with a chain-saw or bow saw at or slightly above the bottom cut of the sink. When the main felling cut is within about 25 mm of the sink, the tree should start to keel over. Step back

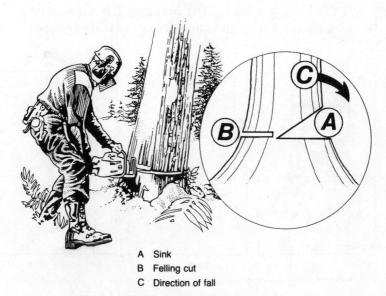

A   Sink
B   Felling cut
C   Direction of fall

Fig. 9.3 Felling cuts.

and to the side and let it fall. If it does not fall do not cut through the 25 mm piece but use a hammer and wedge or breaking bar to topple the tree (Figs. 9.4 and 9.5). Very small trees may be pushed over by hand.

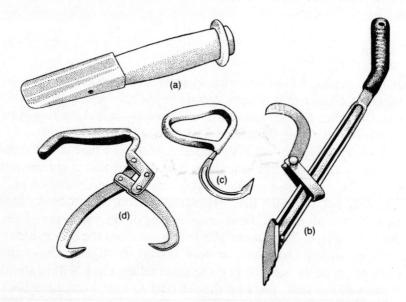

Fig. 9.4 (a) Felling wedge;   (b) breaking bar;   (c) lifting hook for billets and small logs;   (d) lifting tongs.

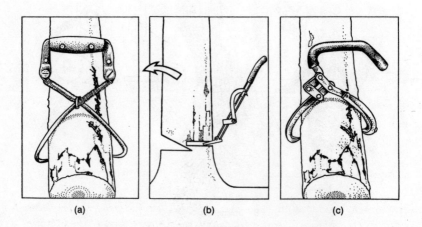

Fig. 9.5 (a) and (c) Two types of handling tongs.   (b) Breaking bar in use.

Avoid standing directly behind the direction of the fall; trees can bounce on their branches and the stem may then slide backwards over the stump. If the tree snags itself against another tree and does not fall to the ground, roll the tree by using a peevie on the butt (Fig. 9.6) or pull it backwards by hand or tractor winch. On no account do anything which involves getting, or putting any other person, under the hanging tree.

Fig. 9.6 Taking down with cant hook (peevie).

Trimming the branches(Snedding)

Start from the butt end and remove by axe or chain-saw branches on the top and sides of the tree. Cut off the top at the 7 cm diameter point. Roll the tree over in a direction away from the body and remove the remaining branches.

Extraction to roadside

Farm tractors that are to be used in the forest require modifications to make them fit for the arduous tasks they have to perform (Fig. 9.7). There is a choice between dragging (skidding) the tree to roadside to be cut up (Fig. 9.8) and cutting it up where

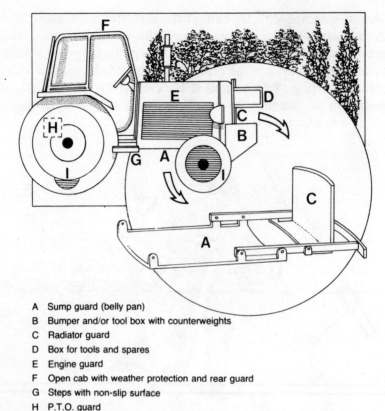

A   Sump guard (belly pan)
B   Bumper and/or tool box with counterweights
C   Radiator guard
D   Box for tools and spares
E   Engine guard
F   Open cab with weather protection and rear guard
G   Steps with non-slip surface
H   P.T.O. guard
I   Tyre valve guards

Fig. 9.7 Farm tractor modifications for forest use.

it lies at stump and then extracting the individual pieces of produce such as sawlogs, pulpwood and fencing posts to roadside (Figs. 9.9 and 9.10).

Extraction of the tree length to roadside can be by winch (usually mounted on a tractor) or by direct attachment by chain or wire sling to a tractor. If a tractor-mounted winch is used, the tractor may be left on or near to a road, and the tree pulled to it; if the distance from roadside to the tree is greater than the length of the winch rope the tractor will have to move off the road towards the tree to be extracted. Once the tree has been hauled up to the tractor, the tractor can be driven to the roadside with the tree. An alternative is to drive the tractor towards the road paying out the winch rope, then to stop the tractor and pull in on

Fig. 9.8 Skidding. (Courtesy J. Airlie Bruce Jones).

Fig. 9.9 Farm tractor with crane and trailer.

Fig. 9.10 Forest tractor forwarder.

the winch rope bringing the tree up to the tractor once more. This manoeuvre can be repeated till the tractor and tree reach the forest road.

If the tree is attached directly to the tractor by a chain or rope it should be as short as possible and hitched to the drawbar so that the end of the tree is clear of the ground.

When pulling, hauling or winching:

(a) never hitch anything to the tractor above the proper drawbar hitch point;
(b) never snatch at a tree, as this could overturn the tractor;
(c) always maintain a steady pull;
(d) always set the tractor in line with the cable;
(e) always be extremely careful if a change of direction is required when hauling;
(f) always make sure that ropes and cables are in good condition and strong enough for the load and that all equipment and couplings are adequate for the work being undertaken.

In all the operations described above involving the use of a tractor there is a greater than normal danger of overturning. For the protection of the operator every tractor used in this type of work should be fitted with a safety cab or frame which has been approved under the Agriculture (Tractor Cabs) Regulations 1974 and have the front weights and other items shown in Fig. 9.7.

If small trees have been cut up at stump the produce may be removed by farm tractor and trailer (Fig. 9.9). Produce from larger trees may well have to be moved on specially built machines. Forestry tractors with trailers, usually steered on the articulated frame principle and equipped with hydraulic cranes, can carry loads of up to ten tonnes over rough terrain. They are

Fig. 9.11 Cable crane. (Courtesy J. Airlie Bruce Jones).

known as forwarders and the movement of prepared produce from stump to roadside is known as forwarding (Fig. 9.10).

In terrain that is too steep for tractors to operate the transport of whole trees or of prepared produce from stump to roadside is undertaken by cable-cranes mounted on modified farm tractors (Fig. 9.11). The setting up and the operation of cableways requires a long period of training and the use of specialised equipment. It is an activity best left to specialist contractors.

Conversion of produce at stump or at roadside

Depending on its size and shape a tree will yield differing proportions of sawlogs and small roundwood such as pulpwood, posts and poles. If the object is to sell such produce then expert advice must be sought on the specifications that have to be cut to meet market requirements and the prices of the different categories of produce. The farmer will himself know the sizes he requires for use on the farm.

The butt cuts are generally the most valuable and so cutting should begin at the butt end with the object of maximising the yield of higher-priced produce.

When cross cutting and stacking produce:

- clear any debris which will interfere with the cross cutting process;
- plan the work so that the lightest produce moves furthest;
- maintain a balanced stance;
- do not stand on the stacked timber;
- ensure that timber is stacked safely (timber stacks should never exceed 2 metres in height);
- when crosscutting with a chain-saw ensure that recommended safe working practice is followed at all times;
- be ready to step back quickly if the log being cut starts to roll;
- stack cut material frequently so that this does not create a hazard underfoot;
- use appropriate aid tools for lifting and moving timber;
- if you are struggling then the material is too heavy–use another method;
- use other logs as a pivot for moving timber;
- keep the back straight when lifting.

Landscape and conservation considerations; timing of operations

Large-scale felling can be unsightly and the quality of the landscape is usually better maintained when felling is done in small groups of half a hectare or less, rather than areas of several hectares. Felling in small groups (coupes) in a wood leaving a matrix of standing trees also helps to retain the forest environment beneficial to plants and animals. If larger scale clear fellings are necessary the actual shape of the area felled is important. Try to avoid rigid rectangular or square shapes and consider the possibility of leaving one or two substantial groups of trees in the foreground. But beware of leaving straggly groups or individual trees on skylines, which should remain either predominantly wooded or predominantly open.

The timing of felling or thinning also needs some thought and the (sometimes conflicting) considerations weighed one against the other. These will include:

- the nesting time for wild or game birds;
- the shooting season for game birds;
- soil conditions for extraction, especially on clay soils;
- timing of extraction or haulage over arable fields;
- availability of labour *vis-a-vis* other farm work if doing one's own tree harvesting;
- timber merchants prefer broadleaves to be winter-felled.

Additional Information

The following are among the relevant leaflets available from the Secretary, Forestry Safety Council, Forestry Commission, 231 Corstorphine Road, Edinburgh EH12 7AT: *The Chain Saw; Chain Saw Snedding; Crosscutting and Stacking; Takedown of Hung-up Trees; and First Aid*.

The Health and Safety Executive, Baynards House, 1 Chepstow Place, London W2 4TF publish an Agricultural Safety series, including: *Safety with Chainsaws* (AS20); *Tree Felling Hauling and Scrubland Clearance* (AS15).

Training

The following organisations are among those which provide training in woodland operations:

Forestry Training Council,
231 Corstorphine Road,
Edinburgh EH12 7AT.

Agricultural Training Board
Bourne House,
32–34 Beckenham Road,
Beckenham,
Kent BR3 4PB.

Local forestry training associations (mainly found in southern England) are listed in local telephone directories.

10   Roads and Tracks

Access to woodlands is needed for inspection, for silvicultural operations, for sporting, for thinning and felling mature timber and for the extraction of timber from stump to farm or public road. Timber extraction puts the greatest demand on tracks and roads and this must always be kept in mind in planning and construction. However, in most woods up to 10 to 20 hectares in extent, all that is required are inspection paths or rides and tractor access. At the other end of the scale large forests need roads capable of carrying lorries of up to 38 tonnes gross laden weight fed by an appropriate system of subsidiary roads or tracks along which forestry forwarders or other similar forestry tractors operate.

Types of forest track and forest road

In practice many different types of track and road are met with but they are mostly variations of one of five basic types:

(1) *Extraction racks*: to take tree lengths or prepared produce to a track or road; just wide enough to take a tractor (e.g. 2.5 metres); made by cutting out one or two rows of trees at intervals of, for example, 20 metres; no ground preparation is required but on soft ground it may be necessary to spread brash in the rack to increase its bearing pressure; almost always straight so as to keep the number of trees removed to a minimum.
(2) *Grass rides*: for general use including extraction of timber; convex shaped cross section to shed water to side drains; generally much wider than racks (e.g. 5 to 6 metres); best in flattish terrain and free-draining soils; no metalling or

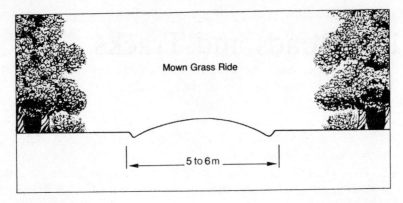

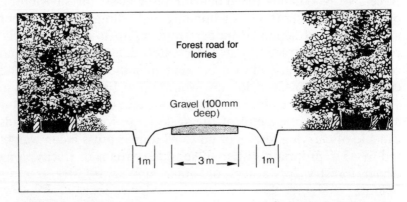

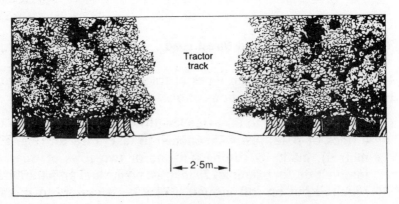

Fig. 10.1 Roads, tracks, rides.

gravelling; rely on grass to bind the surface; regularly mown; good for shooting and nature conservation if well planned and managed.

(3) *Tractor tracks*: general purpose; wide enough to take a tractor (about 3 metres); may involve some earth-moving and digging of drainage ditches and occasional gravelling or metalling; lead from extraction racks to roads, or to woodland boundary in smaller woods under, say, 10 to 20 hectares.
(4) *Estate roads*: existing traditional roads often built for horse-drawn vehicles and farm implements; usually need improvement for modern traffic.
(5) *Forest roads*: capable of taking lorries of up to 38 tonnes gross laden weight; all weather; usually surfaced with gravel or crushed stone; costly to construct and maintain; needed only in large forests.

Typical cross-sections are shown in Fig. 10.1.

The importance of drainage in all grass rides, tracks and roads can hardly be overstated.

Layout and density of forest tracks and roads

In many existing farm woodlands the layout of roads and tracks will be determined by what is already there since abandoning them in favour of a new system can seldom be justified financially. Improvements will consist of strengthening their load-bearing capacity and perhaps adding additional tracks or roads. But, there is no point in building within a woodland a road that is of a higher standard than that with which it connects outside the woodland.

When starting from scratch the principle to be followed is that of a main track or road with spurs leading into the stands. These spurs may be grass rides or tracks.

The intensity of the roads system and the associated tracks is a matter of balancing high capital investment in all weather roads or tracks against lower capital cost tracks and grass rides which may not be usable in all weathers. The balance over the last two decades has shifted away from closely spaced expensive forest roads (a few hundred metres apart) towards very few roads served by tractors travelling on tracks and racks. This is due to the great advances in the design of purpose-built forest tractors capable of high performance across country or on primitive tracks, and in farm forests to the improved performance of agricultural tractors (e.g. 4-wheeled drive and frame steering).

A new road which serves both farm and forest can sometimes be justified on economic grounds when the cost is set against the combined benefits to the two enterprises. A common example is where a tractor track leads from the steading up the hill to and then through the wood and out to grazing land and can be used for timber extraction and to take fertiliser and feed out on the higher pastures.

Generally, before embarking on the layout and construction of roads and tracks advice should be sought from the Forestry Commission, ADAS or private forestry or agricultural consultants with specialised knowledge of the subject. For the farmer who knows what he wants there are contractors in many localities with practical experience in building forest roads.

Maintenance

Drain maintenance is of prime importance. Failure to keep drains running freely will make roads impassable or result in wash-outs. Running surfaces develop ruts and have to be regraded using a mechanical grader or scraper.

Environmental considerations

Where there is a choice of routes to be followed consideration should be given to routes which are the least obtrusive in the landscape. For improvement of nature conservation, cutting more trees than is strictly necessary from the technical point of view along the edges of tracks and roads can often produce the so-called 'edge-effect'. This is beneficial to many forms of wildlife, which make their homes in the safety and shelter of trees and shrubs adjacent to fields or other open ground where they may spend part of the day. The benefits of the edge effect can be increased by good rideside and roadside management, as described below. The loss of production of wood may be compensated for by improvement in the sporting value of the woods.

Management of ridesides and roadsides

In lowland forests especially, the verges of rides and roads can be managed to benefit birds, wild plants and butterflies. A first essential is that the ride or road verges be wide enough to admit sunlight for part of the day and to allow a diversity of shrubs and wild plants to grow on the verges. Cutting out or leaving unplanted 20 metre long bays or scallops on opposite sides of the ride is preferable to having long straight rides of uniform width which tend to be draughty wind-tunnels (Fig. 10.2). As a rough rule of thumb the width of the bays or scallops should be not less than the height of the trees bordering the ride or road. Cutting back the corners at the intersection of rides or roads provides glades where the sun can strike the ground from several angles during the day.

Shrubs should be allowed to colonise areas immediately adjacent to the tree crops, giving way to grasses and herbs nearer the road. Grass swards in front of shrubs should be maintained by

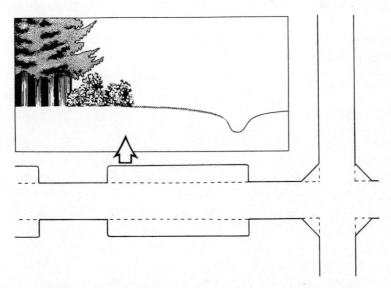

Fig. 10.2 Ride management for conservation showing 20 m long bays or scallops at intervals. Ride intersections, showing cut corners.

mowing or flailing in autumn every two to five years. Shrubs should be cut back every five to seven years and the cut material moved back under the trees.

The rewards can be high in the form of an interesting, diverse plant community supporting a variety of butterflies and other wild creatures. Useful management advice is often available from local naturalist societies.

11 Marketing

Measuring timber

The shape of the main stem or trunk of a tree is that of a tapering cylinder.

In conifers the stem is often straight enough to enable it to be measured right up to near the growing tip of the tree–by convention to 3 inches top diameter (7 cms in the metric system). In broadleaves the main stem tends to get lost in the spreading branches of the crown of the tree, so broadleaves may be measured to 'the spring of the crown'. Exactly where this point is located is often a matter of judgement and is one of the classic causes for dispute between buyer and seller.

Since the stem tapers, volume is measured by:

(a) using the *average* diameter and the formula

$$\text{volume} = \text{length} \times \frac{\pi D^2}{4}$$

 where π is $^{22}\!/_{7}$ or 3.14159 and D is the diameter
 or

(b) using a factor for taper which converts the volume a cylinder as measured by the diameter at the thick end to the real volume of the tree (i.e. the volume of a tapering cylinder). This factor (called the form factor) is obtained from tables which are based on measurements collected over the years by research workers concerned with the art of measuring trees and round wood.

Method (a) or variants of it are normally used for calculating the volume of felled trees or logs because the necessary measurements (length and diameter at the middle point of the tree trunk or log) can be quickly and easily obtained.

Method (b) or variations of it are used for standing trees where it is not practical to measure the diameter at mid-point except with very expensive instruments. Height can be estimated relatively easily.

The practical application of these apparently simple concepts and their extension from individual tree measurement to measurement of whole stands is described in detail in Appendix 3.

Sale of standing trees

In Chapter 9, 'Harvesting Trees', emphasis was placed on the need for training and the use of correct equipment when harvesting trees. It was implied that many farmers would be able to undertake thinning operations and the felling, extraction and conversion of smaller trees, using a power saw and a modified farm tractor with perhaps some simple ancillary equipment like a winch. Certainly this can give employment during slack periods on the farm itself and give the farmer an added interest in and enjoyment from his woods.

Harvesting larger and mature trees calls for equipment and skills of a different order and also poses other questions so that there are fairly strong arguments for selling the timber standing to a timber merchant.

There is the question of capital expenditure on the heavy logging equipment needed to extract and load large trees; then the considerable period of training that is needed in the techniques of felling, de-branching and extracting large trees; and finally the acquisition of knowledge as to how to cross-cut the tree to best economic advantage. A butt worth £100s per cubic metre can be rendered almost worthless if cut to the wrong length (or shattered in felling).

Where a decision has been made to fell or to sell timber it is essential to apply to the Forestry Commission for a felling licence unless the woodland is already covered by a management plan under one of the Forestry Commission grant schemes. The Forestry Commission licence application form will ask for some of the details listed below so it is well to have in mind the needs of both the Forestry Commission and the timber merchant to avoid extra unnecessary work when visiting the wood to make measurements.

Once a licence has been obtained timber merchants should be invited to tender. They will need to have the following information:

- Location: include parish and national grid reference.
- Area: the area to be felled or thinned in hectares.
- Timing: when work is to start and finish.
- Trees to be sold:

  Marking:

  Unless a clear felling is being undertaken the method of marking the individual trees selected for sale should be given (e.g. marked by a blaze or paint spot). The boundaries of areas to be clear-felled must be clearly defined on the ground, and marked on a map.

  Volume:

  If only a few trees are to be sold it will be enough to give for each species the diameter of each tree at 1.3 metres above ground level (breast height diameter) using a girthing tape that reads diameters. For sales of over (say) 50 trees it will probably pay to have a professional assessment of the volume, by species and diameter classes. For those wishing to do their own measurement, methods used are described in Appendix 3.

  Inspection:

  Dates when the site may be visited by prospective purchasers, telephone number of seller or agent and time when available.

  Constraints:

  Any constraints which may affect rate of working or times of working such as sporting interests or wild bird nesting times.

  Access:

  An indication of access to and within the wood. Although access will have to be detailed in the contract it is as well to give merchants at this stage any information which they need to value the timber on offer.

Lists of purchasers of both felled and standing timber may be obtained from the British Timber Merchants' Association, and the Home Timber Merchants' Association of Scotland. Not all timber merchants are members of these associations, so it is well to check entries in the 'Yellow Pages' of the telephone directory.

If the volume of timber to be sold is relatively large (e.g. in excess of 400 cubic metres) it might be worth placing an advertisement in an appropriate periodical such as *Forestry and British Timber* or *The Timber Trades Journal*.

A legally binding contract should be drawn up covering the sale. It must spell out clearly the time of starting and completing the contract, for 'time is of the essence'. The point at which the property in the trees passes to the purchaser must be defined: normally this should be when the tree has been severed from the ground and paid for–implying that the purchaser pays for the trees in advance of his felling them. To avoid asking the purchaser to lay out substantial sums of money in advance of felling, payment in advance can be made in instalments geared to the rate of working achieved in practice.

It is important to note, however, that in standing sales the sale must be made for *the number of trees*, not the volume, because of the difficulty in guaranteeing the measurement of the volume of standing trees (see Appendix 4). The contract must then describe the timber to be sold and how marked, repeating the information under marking and volume in the tender form (see above).

In addition to the above it should make provision for:

(a) Purchaser's liability for repairs to gates, fences, walls, roads and ditches resulting from harvesting and transport operations; for the treatment of stumps with a chemical as a protection against root rot in the remaining trees (conifers only).
(b) Purchaser's liability for damage to trees not included in the sale, e.g. damage done by the purchaser during extraction. Penalty for felling trees not included in the sale.
(c) Non-disturbance of sporting and conservation interests and other constraints, e.g. prohibition of Sunday working.
(d) Extension of time allowed for completion of the contract due to delays resulting from unavoidable circumstances such as unfavourable weather.
(e) Agreed access routes–to be spelt out in detail on a map. Purchaser to satisfy himself as to adequacy of bridges, culverts, etc.
(f) The keeping of and control of animals (e.g. dogs) on the site.

(g) The purchaser's liability under the Health and Safety at Work Act. Purchasers should be insured against liability on their behalf.

(h) Arbitration in the event of disputes.

Sale of felled trees and produce

Ideally, where the felling and extraction is to be undertaken by the farmer and the prepared produce sold at the roadside, details of the sale should be agreed before any felling is undertaken so that the purchaser's views on the best way of cutting up the tree are taken into account. Another good reason for selling produce in advance of felling is that with some species once the tree is felled deterioration of the log can set in, especially during the summer months. Not only can damage be caused by fungi (this can be severe in pines, Douglas fir and the light-coloured hardwoods such as beech), but the logs may be also prone to attack by wood boring insects. Methods of measurement of trees for sale are given in Appendix 3.

Examples of agreements for standing sales and of logs felled by the owner

The Forestry Commission sell much of their timber by competitive tender or at auction. A contract exists when a tender is accepted by the Commission or an auction bid is accepted by the auctioneer on behalf of the Commission. *Memoranda of Agreement* are then signed. Examples of Memoranda of Agreement for Sale of Standing Trees and Standard Conditions of Sale and of the corresponding documents for sales of logs felled by the Commission are given in Appendix 4. The authors and publishers wish to thank the Forestry Commission for kindly supplying copies of these documents which are based on the Commission's experience of selling timber built up over some forty years.

Main markets

The main markets for timber in Britain are described below by types of industry–wood processing (e.g. pulp mills), sawmilling, veneer and fuelwood.

The wood processing industries

Roundwood is in continuous demand by pulp mills for the manufacture of paper and cardboard and by particle board (chipboard) mills in many parts of Britain. New products such as medium density fibreboard (MDF) and oriented strand board (OSB) are also made from small diameter roundwood in Britain.

There is a wide variety of acceptable species and dimensions, and these are subject to change as the various units instal new equipment. *It is therefore essential to obtain an up-to-date specification before preparing roundwood for these markets.*

At one time it was difficult for the small producer to sell into these markets but there are now few parts of the country without someone willing to buy from the small owner. The local Forestry Commission office is usually able to put farmers in touch with the individual firms or organisations active in a locality.

There are some locally important markets such as those for turnery poles; for round stake production; and for pokers for smelting works.

The sawmilling industry

The sawmilling industry is usually able to offer substantially higher prices for material of sawlog size than are the various wood-processing industries. A number of sawmills specialise in sawing for particular markets, such as panel fencing or pallets, and this enables them to use logs of smaller diameters than those needed to produce construction and furniture timbers. If an owner has trees that will yield logs of a minimum size of three metres length with a minimum top diameter of 12 to 15 cms he should find out what are the species and sizes required by sawmills in the locality. The 'Yellow Pages' of the telephone directory under *sawmills* and *timber merchants* will provide local addresses but to ensure full coverage of potential buyers it may be helpful to get names of purchasers of sawlogs from the Forestry Commission local office or the merchants' associations.

Veneer logs

Large diameter clean boles of a number of species, including ash, cherry, oak, sycamore, walnut and yew can command very high prices if they are of veneer quality.

Fuelwood

Widespread sales of wood-burning stoves during the past two decades have stimulated the demand for all types of firewood in Britain, and while this tends to be an intermittent market, it is not one which should be ignored.

The heavier hardwoods such as beech, birch, ash, oak and hornbeam burn less rapidly than the lower density species, including the conifers. They generate more heat because their higher densities mean that more wood substance is available per unit volume of fuel. Poplar burns less satisfactorily than other species, and larch should only be used in a fully enclosed stove because it is liable to 'spit'.

The fuel value of most species is around 18,000,000 joules per kilogramme (i.e. 7800 British thermal units per lb). Weight for weight the calorific value of coal is twice as great, and that of fuel oil is two and one half times higher.

Although green wood has a positive calorific value, the presence of so much water makes it difficult to ignite because the access of oxygen is impeded and the heat needed to drive out the water reduces its efficiency by about 25 per cent. Fuel wood should therefore be left in the open to dry during the spring and summer months, and then stored under cover.

Timber quality and value

As a general rule the value of timber increases in proportion to size. This is illustrated in Fig. 11.1, which is derived from published figures for sales of standing conifers by the Forestry Commission for year ending 31 March 1986. The absolute figures for price have not much relevance to the prices that may be obtained for individual parcels of timber sold standing from farm woodland, but the relative values of the different sizes of tree will hold good.

There is a distinct variation, with prices in Scotland falling below those in England and Wales. Within this general pattern prices vary from year to year depending on the demand for particular products. Particular circumstances, such as severe gales bringing a lot of windthrown timber onto the market, can distort prices further.

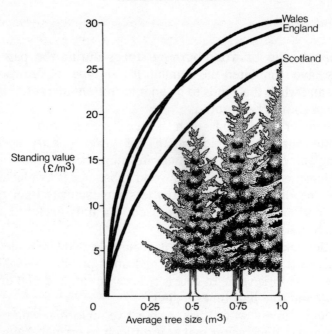

Fig. 11.1 Price/size curve for conifers, showing how the value
       of the timber rises with size.

Timber quality

Good quality timber always fetches a better price than poor
quality but what makes for good quality? A timber merchant
wants to saw out of a log the longest possible piece of squared
timber with the biggest diameter he can get. So a good log has to
be straight, long and must not taper too rapidly. Knots, if any,
should be small and there should be no old scars or signs of decay.
Nor should there be any sign of insect damage, or of staining of
the wood seen at the end of the log. There should be no metal
e.g. nails or fence wire embedded in the wood. There should be
no splits in the wood. Some broadleaved species particularly oak
and chestnut develop splits or 'shakes', usually on dry sites, and
these may go for some distance up the stem. The cracks may
radiate from the centre of the log ('star shake' found frequently in
oak) or they may follow one of the annual growth rings partly or
completely round the log ('ring shake' found mainly in sweet
chestnut). Conifers sometimes develop cracks too; they are most

likely to be found in grand fir and noble fir. The presence of a shake may sometimes be inferred from a narrow scar running vertically up the trunk (or at a slight angle to the vertical) on a standing tree.

Decay

The main types of decay to look out for are conifer heart rot and pipe rot. The former, also called Fomes rot after the fungus which causes it (recently renamed Heterobasidion) attacks conifers, although Douglas fir and silver firs are relatively resistant. The rot comes in through wounds or from infected roots and can travel up the stem for several metres, causing first a dark stain and then decay. Pipe rot or Stereum rot attacks mainly oak. It affects the heartwood and enters through wounds or broken and dead branches. Any oak with dead branches in the crown may be affected. On a tree which has been felled and trimmed, its presence can be seen by blackening of the heartwood of the branches, sometimes as a black ring and sometimes as a hole. The rot travels into the heartwood of the stem, and may eventually hollow it out.

Species and value

Among conifers there is some variation of price between species, with pine usually at the lower end and Douglas fir and good larch at the upper end, although this may vary from region to region. The graph gives a broad indication of the standing value of whole trees in 1986. Locally, prices will vary considerably.

Price guide for broadleaves

Among broadleaves the highest prices are paid for timber with decorative grain provided the logs are of sufficient size to be cut for veneer. The most prized timbers are walnut, oak, cherry, ripple-grained sycamore and yew (a conifer). Veneer logs must be straight and cylindrical with no grooves ('fluting'), knots, old wounds or blemishes of any sort. The minimum length required is usually 3 metres and the diameter should be as large as possible.

For oak this means at least 60 cm, but other species may be acceptable down to 30–40 cm. A guide to price is £120–£220 per cubic metre.

A guide to prices in the principal markets for broadleaves not of veneer quality is given below, by species. The price guides given are those which might be expected standing in normal market conditions in England, where the bulk of hardwood sawmills are situated. Somewhat lower prices should be expected in Scotland and in some parts of Wales where conifer forestry predominates. The prices are intended to show the *relative* values, not absolute values which change with time and place.

Oak

After veneer quality logs, the next most valuable category is called planking oak. The standard required is nearly as high as for veneer logs and it should be winter-felled. Logs should be straight, free from knots, shake or rot with a minimum diameter of 45 cm and minimum length of 2 m. Price guide: £50–£100 per cubic metre for that part of the tree that will yield planking material.

Fencing quality oak is used for sawn posts, feather-edged boarding and rails. It should be reasonably straight and free from serious shake or rot. Small knots are acceptable for boards and rails; larger knots for posts. Minimum diameter 30 cm. Price guide: £25–£35 per cubic metre.

Mining timber is sawn into blocks (or chocks) for use in mines, and rough knotty timber is acceptable. Minimum diameter 20 cm, minimum length 1 m. Price guide: £12–£18 per cubic metre. (This is a declining market.)

Ash

Ash should be felled in winter and the logs moved quickly to the sawmill for conversion. The wood must be white in colour. Larger sizes, over 40 cm diameter are used for furniture. Price guide: £40–£90 per cubic metre. Smaller sizes, 20–40 cm are used for tool handles. Price guide: £30–£35 per cubic metre. Anything which does not meet these grades will go for mining timber.

Beech

If left in the log beech timber discolours and decays quickly, so must be felled in winter and moved rapidly to the sawmill for conversion and drying (seasoning). Furniture quality should be free of knots and rot and white in colour. Minimum diameter 30 cm. Price guide: £30–£40 per cubic metre. In some places, smaller sized beech is used for turnery in diameters of 20 to 40 cm. Price guide: £10–£20 per cubic metre. Poor quality material is acceptable for mining timber.

Sycamore

This is a white wood which must be winter-felled and moved quickly to the sawmill for conversion to boards which are stacked on end for seasoning. Large boles which will yield clean logs, over 40 cm diameter, fetch prices similar to ash, i.e. £40–£90 per cubic metre.

Chestnut

The timber of older trees may be useless, except as firewood, because of shake, but sound clean boles of 50 cm diameter or more can fetch £50–£100 per cubic metre. Coppice poles, 7–10 cm diameter, are used for fencing stakes. Chestnut coppice is an important crop in SE England, where it is sold by area at annual auctions for cleft fencing and hop poles at prices up to £1500 per hectare for the best quality well-stocked areas.

Turnery

Turnery markets are local and prices will depend on the distance to the mill. Species taken are usually birch, sycamore, alder and sometimes beech and ash. The diameter is 8–25 cm and lengths usually are about 2 m. Price guide: £2–£9 per cubic metre for straight and clean pole material.

Pulpwood

The market for broadleaved pulpwood is mainly in the south of Britain, and prices will depend on the distance from the mill. The diameter range is 5–40 cm and the billets must be reasonably straight, in lengths of 1.2 or 2 m. Any species is acceptable. Price guide: £2–£8 per cubic metre for standing poles that will yield pulpwood.

Firewood

Since wood-burning stoves became popular, a firewood market has developed in most parts of the country within reach of centres of population. Any broadleaved species is acceptable although ash, oak and beech are preferred; the roughest material can be used. Price guide: £2–£8 per cubic metre.

Woodland produce other than timber

Markets exist for woodland produce other than timber. The most profitable of these is the ornamental foliage of evergreen species such as silver fir, western hemlock, western red cedar, Lawson's cypress, Norway spruce and holly, which may be sold by weight to florists and wreath-makers. Additionally, the tops of some coniferous species are marketable as Christmas trees; silver fir and Norway spruce are the best for this purpose, but in some localities pines, Douglas fir and Sitka spruce are acceptable. It may therefore pay to time the felling of these species to coincide with the pre-Christmas period. The local Forestry Commission office may be able to help with the names of Christmas tree merchants. Where the number of Christmas trees available is relatively small, farm gate sales direct to the public might be considered.

12 Management for Nature Conservation

Any woodland, even a pure conifer plantation, provides a habitat for wildlife, and the range of species which it will support will be different from that of the surrounding farmland. A wood is rather like a block of flats, with different inhabitants on each floor. For example, nightjars nest on the ground, wrens and warblers on low shrubs, thrushes and finches in tall shrubs, and woodpigeons and rooks in the crowns of trees. The 'floors' or 'layers' which are usually distinguished are the *tree canopy*, consisting of the crowns of the trees, the *understorey*, consisting of smaller-growing or possibly younger trees, the *shrub layer*, the *field layer* (herb layer, or ground flora) consisting of non-woody plants, and the *litter layer* consisting of the debris on the forest floor. To provide the best possible home for wildlife, all of these layers should be present in some degree, and the woodland should be managed so as to perpetuate them all, although they do not all need to be present on the same piece of ground.

Normal forest management will produce each in turn. A well-stocked mature wood may not have much in the way of a shrub layer or a field layer. When it is felled, the field layer develops rapidly from seeds lying dormant in the soil, and the site becomes rich in characteristic woodland plants, and in the insects and small animals which live on and among them. Planted trees grow up, along with natural seedlings of trees and shrubs, and within 5 to 10 years form a shrub layer which may be so dense as to shade out the ground flora almost completely. The forester, by cleaning the plantation (i.e. by cutting out unwanted woody growth) may keep the field layer going for a few years longer, until the crop trees themselves form a thicket. By the time the trees have grown big enough to produce useful poles from thinnings, a tree canopy will have developed, and the operation of thinning will let in more light and a limited ground flora will reappear.

If nature conservation is the principal objective, the best way of regenerating a wood (i.e. replacing one mature timber crop with another) is not by clear felling, but by felling small areas of perhaps 0.2 to 0.5 hectare at intervals of 5 to 10 years. In this way the animals and birds, which depend on a particular stage in the development of a tree crop, can always find a home. Some species, particularly some types of lichen, can only live on mature trees, and so it is undesirable to fell all the mature trees before there are others approaching a mature stage. If economic or other considerations go against this method of regeneration, then it should be done by felling in stages as far as possible, and some groups of mature trees should be retained. These will act as reservoirs or refuges, from which the species which depend on mature trees can recolonise the wood, as favourable conditions again develop. These groups could consist of the rougher and less valuable trees, and should include some dead or dying ones, which in their turn are 'home' to a variety of insects and fungi.

Tree species vary in the range of wildlife which they will support, and in this respect most native trees support a bigger range of species of wildlife than trees which have been introduced by man. The British Trust for Conservation Volunteers recorded 284 insect species associated with oak and only 15 with sycamore. Similarly, Scots pine–a native–had 91 but larch, introduced in the seventeenth century from Europe, had only 17.

The most valuable woods for nature conservation are those described as ancient semi-natural woods. 'Ancient' woodland sites are those which are thought to have been continuously wooded since at least 1600 AD. Ancient semi-natural woodland, as well as having been under trees for centuries consists of trees and shrubs native to the site, and is the nearest link we have to the natural forest which covered Britain in prehistoric times. The Nature Conservancy Council has prepared a register of ancient woodland, which can be consulted at offices of the Nature Conservancy or the Forestry Commission or the local Planning Authority. Copies are also held by Regional Secretaries of Timber Growers UK and the Country Landowners' Association, two organisations which promote the interests of private woodland owners.

In 1985 the Government announced a national policy for broadleaved woodland. The essentials of this are incorporated in the new March 1988 Woodland Grant Scheme (WGS). Broadleaved woods cannot be cleared unless they are replanted for another broadleaved crop, and the planting of new broadleaved woods, and the management of existing ones is to be encouraged. Ancient semi-natural woods should receive special management to preserve their nature conservation value. In particular large areas should not be clear felled, and species which are not native to the site should not be introduced.

In planting a crop of a slow-growing broadleaf such as oak, there is an old-established practice of mixing the main crop species with a faster-growing one to act as a 'nurse'. The nurse species, usually a conifer, becomes established quickly providing shelter for the main species and helping to draw it up. The nurse must be removed in the course of thinning before it starts to dominate the plantation and harm the main species. This gives an earlier return from the sale of thinnings than could be expected if the main species had been planted alone.

Now that there is a market for small broadleaved poles, as firewood or pulpwood, there is, perhaps, little need to use conifer as a nurse in southern Britain. A fast-growing broadleaf could be used instead, such as alder which has the additional benefit of being able to 'fix' nitrogen from the air, in the same way as peas or beans. Conifer nurses still have a place on frosty or exposed sites and in the uplands, and they may be accepted for replanting ancient semi-natural sites provided they do not exceed 25 per cent of the planted stock. Scots pine, European larch or Norway spruce may be appropriate, and they must be removed before they adversely affect the growth of the broadleaved species. (The financial benefits of using a conifer nurse must be weighed against the lower conifer grant and it may often be found that a completely broadleaved plantation is the better proposition.)

A new requirement of the 1988 WGS is that conifer plantings will be required to have an element of broadleaves.

A traditional form of forest management, coppice with standards, which dates from mediaeval times, is considered to be a good system for combining environmental benefits with wood production. Coppice is a crop derived by cutting trees at ground level and allowing new shoots to grow from the stumps. It can easily be recognised in a wood by the clusters of poles arising from one spot, even though the old stump may have rotted away. Coppice was traditionally cut on a rotation of up to 25 years for firewood, or charcoal-making or for poles for fencing or light construction work. Hazel coppice was cut for hazel hurdles, bean and pea sticks, thatching spars and hedging rods at 8 to 12 years of age.

Coppice, then, regularly recreates the conditions for a good field layer, followed by a shrub layer and an understorey, but it never produces a tall tree canopy. Nor, of course, does coppice produce any large sized timber but this can be remedied by growing isolated trees as standards over the coppice. Standards are usually of oak, and may be introduced by planting in gaps among the coppice. The gaps should be at least 6 m across to give the plants a chance of survival against the strong competition of the coppice regrowth. Alternatively, good stems are selected at the time the coppice is cut, and are left standing. They should preferably be 'maidens' (i.e. trees which have developed from seedlings) rather than 'stool shoots' (i.e. shoots from cut stumps). Eventually these will reduce the vigour and productivity of the coppice beneath them. With oak standards on a fairly good site, sixty standards, of all ages, per hectare will produce a canopy which occupies about half the available crown space. Forty standards per hectare will occupy about one third of the crown space.

Native trees which coppice well are alder, ash, hornbeam, lime, oak and willow, as does hazel, a native shrub. Introduced species include sycamore and sweet chestnut, the latter producing commercially valuable crops on suitable soils in the south of England. Three other fast-growing exotic species which will coppice are poplar, nothofagus and eucalyptus. Poplar is not well regarded as firewood because of the high moisture content of the wood when felled, but it could be worth growing for a pulpwood market. The other two species are rather exacting as to site and are liable to damage from frost. They have been grown experimentally as 'biomass coppice' (or 'energy coppice') a field crop harvested on a short rotation of about 5 years, for the production of wood chips for pulp or fuel.

Hurdle making, the main use of hazel coppice, has largely disappeared and the continuing market–pegs for use in thatching to hold the thatch in place–is small relative to the area of hazel coppice still to be found in southern England. So in general, the revenue from coppice other than sweet chestnut will depend mainly on the firewood market.

It is possible to improve the nature conservation value of commercial woodland by following a few simple principles. Wide rides, 10 metres or more in width, permit the survival of ground flora species. Bays cut along tracks or roads, corners cut away at road or ride intersections, all help by letting in sunlight and encouraging shrub adjacent to the trees and then a herb layer. Both sides of a ride, track or road should not be mown each year. Cutting in alternate years will permit the flowering of brambles and other species necessary for some butterflies, and will also give suitable conditions for ground-nesting birds. Wet areas in the wood (which are often difficult to drain and to grow trees on) should be left in a natural state. Stream sides should not be planted, but should be left open to an overall width of ten times the width of the stream and never less than 20 metres. Herbicides should be used with care, and spot application is preferable to overall spraying. In designing planting schemes more than one tree species should be used. This is best done by including groups of a second species among the main one. If the main species is a shade-bearer, the secondary species should be a light demander. In any planting scheme it is reasonable to include a small proportion (5 to 10 per cent by number) of 'conservation species' e.g. wild service tree, crab apple, rowan, field maple. These should preferably be planted at the woodland edge or around clearings or at ride-sides. Hedges around the woodland should be maintained, as they help to replace the shrub layer if it is missing. It might be possible to leave some open areas in the wood for occasional use as stacking sites for timber.

The watchword is 'diversity'. The more variety of species, ages and types of woodland, the better for the wildlife.

13 Management for Sport

Pheasants

Management for sport usually refers to pheasants and a carefully planned woodland can improve the value of a farm and bring in a significant income from the shooting rent or give pleasurable sporting in winter. Partridge which are field and hedgerow birds are being bred on some shoots and in the sporting sense they complement pheasant which are essentially woodland birds. The partridge shooting season starts on the first of September, a month earlier than the pheasant season.

Although pheasant are not native, the principles already given for nature conservation management apply. Pheasants need shelter from wind at ground level, which can be provided by a good perimeter hedge, by young plantations, coppice or groups of young trees within the wood. They also need shelter for roosting; this is often provided by evergreen conifers. They need sunlight, which they can get in wide rides, or permanent glades, or on areas cut for coppices or for replanting. Such places also provide low cover for nesting, e.g. bramble. Native shrubs and small-growing trees planted at ride sides or on the woodland edge provide natural food. The tree crop should include oak, and, among conifers, some larch to prevent the wood being too dark. The planting of shrubs which are not native should perhaps be avoided (with the possible exception of *lonicera* which can be kept under control with a swipe). On no account should rhododendron be planted; it can become a serious hindrance to effective woodland management because it spreads rapidly and forms a dense cover which prevents regeneration and makes replanting difficult.

Pheasants are not strong fliers, and prefer to fly downhill and with a following wind. So in planning a shoot, the woods should be about 200 to 500 metres apart and preferably on elevated ground so that the guns can stand below them on the line of flight to the next wood. A good arrangement is to have a largish central wood with a ring of smaller coverts round it. Birds released in the centre wood will disperse to the outer ones, but will tend to fly back to it when driven. It is important to consider the direction in which birds will be driven in each wood and to provide flushing points at suitable places. The essentials of a flushing point are to have tall trees at the edge of the wood so that the birds fly high over the guns (Fig. 13.1). Inside this, the trees should be cleared or heavily thinned out, for a distance equal to the height of the edge trees, or rather more. This gives the pheasants room to gain height. The ground may be used for a low-growing crop such as coppice or Christmas trees, but the height of the crop should be graded down to low shrubs at the inner side. An angle of 30 degrees is ideal. From this point back into the wood there should be patches of low shrubs to hold the birds as the beaters drive them forward.

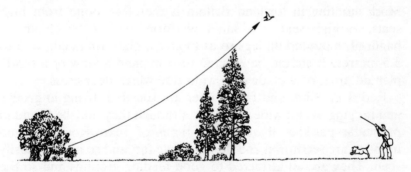

Fig. 13.1 Flushing point. Tall trees to get birds to fly high.

Forest operations should be planned with the needs of the shoot in mind. Firstly there is a need for good access for keepering, and the woods themselves must be passable for beaters. This will probably entail some brashing and cutting of racks not strictly required for forest management purposes. The greatest conflict of interests can occur in early summer, especially from mid-May to the end of June, when the pheasants are nesting in young plantations which urgently need weeding. The problem can be

avoided by using soil-acting herbicides, such as propyzamide,
which are applied in winter. Another time to avoid disturbance is
in early autumn at the start of the shooting season, and thinning
or felling should not be programmed for this period. Felling
should be planned a year or more in advance so that a wood
where felling is due to take place may be left out of the shoot for
that year and the pheasants encouraged to breed in other woods.

Deer

Deer are present in many woodlands, and numbers have
increased as a result of new planting over the last 30–40 years.
They can do serious damage to trees by browsing and bark-
stripping in winter, and by the males cleaning their antlers in
summer. The damage may be reduced by careful management
and culling (i.e. planned reduction of numbers) and a nuisance
converted to a sporting asset. As deer are shot with a rifle, public
safety demands that the stalker should shoot from a position
where the bullet will go into the ground if it misses the target.
Most shooting in lowland Britain is therefore done from high
seats. A high seat is a small platform, with a bench and a
handrail, mounted on legs so as to give a platform height of 3 to
3.5 metres. It should be erected to command a view of a newly
planted area, or a glade or a wide ride which deer cross.

Red deer, sika, and fallow deer are sociable, living in groups
and ranging over a wide territory, although they may be found in
particular parts of it at certain times of year. Roe deer and
muntjac are territorial and do not move far, and so are less easily
seen. They are all attracted to good feeding grounds and so the
creation and maintenance of good glades is an essential part of the
woodland management. Glades should be 0.2–1.0 hectare in size
and their locations should be chosen before planting, if possible;
suitable sites are in sheltered valleys, along streamsides, in areas
of fairly open mature broadleaves or areas of good grass,
especially old agricultural land. Any areas being used by deer
should be made into glades even if this means abandoning a
damaged tree crop. Dense tree crops at the edges of glades
should be thinned out and brashed. Willow and rowan planted in
the glades will provide browse, and, if necessary, small patches of

ground of 500 square metres or more may be reseeded with a grass clover mixture to give better grazing.

Co-operation with neighbours is advisable in planning the management of wide-ranging species of deer, which may move from one owner's land to another's.

The Game Conservancy, Fordingbridge, Hants, publishes a series of useful booklets on game management, and also provides an advisory service, for which a charge is made.

14 Management for Landscape and Amenity

Skylines

Trees and woods are important in the landscape, particularly when they form the skyline. In lowland Britain, hills generally have rounded tops, and the rounded crowns of broadleaved trees seem to fit in naturally. Not so the spiky tops of conifer trees. If a conifer wood appears on the skyline it has a silhouette like the teeth of a saw, which looks out of place among rounded hills, although it may fit in well with rugged mountainous scenery. (The exception is Scots pine which develops a rounded top as it matures.) In planning woodland, then, it is important to consider the skyline and if appropriate to keep conifers lower down the hill. A crown of long-lived broadleaves, such as oak, at the top of a wood will last for several rotations of conifers, and although it may not produce much in the way of timber, the environmental benefits may well compensate for the loss of production.

Boundaries

When laying out a new plantation, or dividing up an existing wood, it is tempting to use straight lines because these are easy to mark on the ground, and to survey on to a map. The result in the landscape looks unnatural and has been the cause of much criticism in the past. Boundaries both external and internal (i.e. rides or the division between different crops) should not be straight, and ideally should follow the natural form of the land. A useful idea which has been developed by the Forestry Commission's landscape architects is that there are 'lines of force' in the landscape. This can be used to help produce more natural shapes in woodland in hilly districts. Put very simply, one has to imagine that there are forces pushing *upwards* in valleys or gullies, towards the top of the hill, and that there are other forces pushing *downwards* on shoulders or ridges. If you allow your boundary to be distorted in response to these imaginary forces, you will get a more natural-looking line which will fit better into the landscape (Fig. 14.1).

For example, it is intended to plant a hillside which has two or three streams running down it in shallow gullies (or re-entrants) with low ridges between them. For silvicultural reasons larch is to be planted below the 100 metre contour line and pine above. To make the contour line the exact species boundary would give an artificial looking firm line across the hillside. But if the boundary between the larch and the pine is allowed to be influenced by the lines of force, allowing it to go higher than 100 metres in the re-entrants and lower than 100 metres on the ridges, the result is a

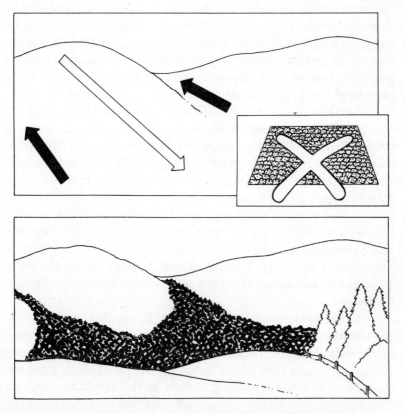

Fig. 14.1 Plantation shape as influenced by 'lines of force' in the landscape.

wavy line which emphasises the underlying land form. If, in addition the two crops are planted so that some larch runs into the pine and vice versa, the effect is more natural-looking than an abrupt change from one species to the other.

The same principle can be used to design the shape of a new wood, or of a felling area within a wood. Truly natural boundaries such as rock faces or water courses can sometimes be used. For economy and ease of fencing, or to avoid creating traps for sheep in bad weather, it may be necessary to fence outside the carefully designed boundary (do not be tempted to plant up to the fence).

Mixing tree species

For silvicultural or economic reasons it is often argued that it is desirable to mix two or more species in a plantation; broadleaved species are planted with a faster growing conifer to act as a 'nurse', by giving shelter and establishing woodland conditions quickly. The conifer produces usable poles sooner than the broadleaf, and is gradually removed in thinning to leave a broadleaved crop, although many foresters would wish to keep a few of the conifers on to maturity for economic reasons. The economic argument is questionable in those parts of the country where there is a ready market for small broadleaved poles as firewood or pulpwood, and where small parcels of conifer thinnings are difficult to sell. Moreover, current grant schemes give a higher rate of grant for plantings consisting solely of broadleaves, and any admixture of conifers automatically brings more intensive management to ensure that the objectives of the mixture are achieved. This entails additional time for the owner-manager or additional costs if a professional management firm is employed.

The simplest method of mixing a conifer nurse with a broadleaved species is to plant bands of the two species alternately, usually three rows of each. This can be thinned by taking out whole rows of the faster growing species. It produces a pattern of unnatural-looking stripes in the landscape and so is best avoided, unless the terrain is flat so that it cannot be seen. A better appearance is produced by planting groups of one species in a matrix of the other. The simplest way is to plant three rows of the conifer alternating with three rows which consist of groups of the conifer and the broadleaf. For example, a common mixture for Norway spruce and oak is to have three rows of spruce, alternating with three rows in which nine plants of oak alternate with nine plants of spruce giving a proportion of three spruce to one oak. Silviculturally, the larger the group of the slower tree the better and the minimum size of group should be 25 plants. At this size the group is likely to be successful even if the plantation is neglected, and thinning of the faster growing conifer is delayed for any reason. But even this arrangement gives an artificial-looking appearance to the wood. A more natural appearance can be achieved by planting irregularly shaped groups or 'drifts' of one species in a matrix of the other. These can be from 50 to 250 plants in size. Management is somewhat more difficult, especially if hand weeding is required, since the weeders do not know when to expect a change of species. A possible solution is to use a granular herbicide, such as propyzamide applied in winter when it is easier to see the young trees. Groups of the faster-growing species should be arranged so that they may be thinned and the produce extracted without having to damage the slower species which will not be ready for thinning until later.

A 'natural' mix can sometimes be achieved by using vegetation changes visible on the site, e.g. by planting larch in the bracken patches, spruce on the rushy areas and so on.

It is often not strictly necessary to have a conifer as a nurse, and a fast growing broadleaf such as alder can be used. The various species of alder are particularly useful on difficult sites such as the reclamation of old mineral workings, as they are able to 'fix' nitrogen for themselves.

Mixed woodland can be scenically more attractive than a 'monoculture' or single species wood. Where the species grow at about the same rate, they can be mixed intimately, e.g. Scots pine and European larch, or ash and sycamore. An advantage of having species with different growth rates, and hence different rotation lengths, is that one will mature before the other so that clear felling of the whole wood is avoided. The groups of later maturing trees should be planned so that, when exposed by the felling, they will have a pleasing shape, and are so placed in relation to roads or rides that they can be felled later without damaging the new crop on the cleared area. Examples of species which might be mixed in this way are oak (100–120 years or more), beech (80–100 years), ash, sycamore, Norway maple (60–80 years) and wild cherry (50–60 years).

Even a small proportion of broadleaves, as little as 10–15 per cent by area, can be valuable in improving the appearance of conifer woodland. They should be planted in groups to enhance natural features such as gullies or rocky outcrops, to reinforce natural scrub, or to link up with broadleaves outside the woodland boundary, such as hedgerow trees. There is something to be said for planting the broadleaves on the poorer parts of the site. The loss to commercial timber production in the main crop is less, and because the broadleaves will grow more slowly on a poor site, their environment effect will last longer. Broadleaves too, can give a much more pleasing skyline than conifers in the lowlands.

Felling retentions

When a uniform tree crop matures, it is simplest to clear fell, but this is often not acceptable on amenity or environmental grounds. It then becomes necessary to retain some trees, either to screen the felled area from some particular viewpoint, or to provide a feature of interest in the felled area. Leaving trees standing around the edge will give a reasonable screen on flat land, but looks artificial on a slope. Keeping a scattering of trees over the whole area gives a pleasing effect resembling parkland. The disadvantage is that the crowns of the retained trees spread and affect the growth of new crop. Nor can they be felled and removed without causing damage to the young trees. Trees for retention in this way should, if possible, be young, well-formed stems, which will last for at least the greater part of the lifetime of the new crop. Alternatively, a few moribund trees may be left to provide wildlife habitats.

On a hillside which is viewed mainly from below, a felling can be screened by leaving belts of trees parallel with the contours, as well as the trees on the lower edge of the wood. It is better from the amenity point of view not to leave trees isolated on the skyline, in a position where the viewer sees the gap between the tree crowns and the ground. In any case, trees isolated in this way often die back rapidly.

A natural feature, such as a rockface, in a felled area, can be made into a point of interest by retaining trees beside and above it as a 'frame'.

Colour in the crop

Spring and autumn colours in deciduous crops are obviously important for amenity, but it is not always realised that there are considerable colour differences in conifer foliage which can give variety, particularly in winter. A guide to colour for some commonly planted species is given below.

Conifers

Dark greens: Douglas fir, western hemlock, Sitka spruce, grand fir, Corsican pine.
Lighter greens: Norway spruce, lodgepole pine, red cedar (bronze in winter), Lawson's cypress (ornamental varieties range from gold to blue), larch (deciduous, pale green in spring, yellow in autumn).
Bluish greens: Scots pine, noble fir.

Broadleaves

Species	Spring colour	Autumn colour
Ash	pale green	yellow-brown
Beech	pale green	orange-brown
Norway maple	pale green	bright yellow
Oak	yellowish green	golden-brown
Red oak	yellowish green	red-brown
Poplar	pale green	yellow
Sycamore	pale green	dull brown
Whitebeam	white	brown
Wild cherry	pale green (white blossom)	red-brown

15 Shelter Belts

Shelter belts can serve several purposes. They can:

- provide shelter for livestock from cold winds, rain and snow storms, especially at critical times like lambing;
- improve the growing conditions for crops;
- provide summer shade for stock;
- provide shelter for houses and buildings;
- improve sporting and wildlife.

A properly managed shelter belt can also provide timber for use on the farm or for sale.

The need for shelter varies greatly from farm to farm. Although windblow of light soils and fen peats occurs at or near sea level, as a general rule the need for shelter increases with increased elevation.

On some upland farms livestock are fed within woodlands during the winter or given shelter within woodlands in severe weather. This can result in damage to the woodland by bark stripping and on some soils by 'poaching' (soil compaction); these troubles are made worse by high stocking densities. On hard dry soils (e.g. moraines) in older tree crops, moderate densities of cattle do little damage where adequate feed is provided.

The effectiveness of a shelter belt in reducing wind forces is a function of its height, width and density.

A dense impenetrable belt gives the greatest reduction in wind force but this effect occurs only for a relatively short distance in the lee of the belt–commonly some 10–15 times the height of the belt. A shelter belt which allows some wind to penetrate through it reduces the wind force on the lee side for distances up to 30 times its height and creates less turbulence (Fig. 15.1).

For livestock the most effective shelter belt is either a dense belt or a more open belt of trees reinforced at ground level by a

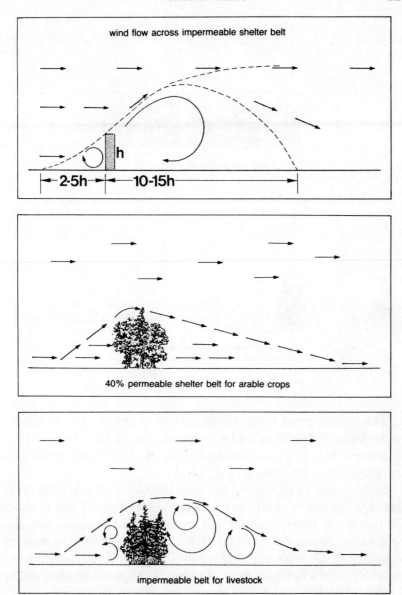

Fig. 15.1 Two types of shelterbelt: impermeable and permeable.

layer of shrubs to give a dense barrier (Fig. 15.3). For promoting grass or other crop growth or for reducing soil blow the less dense belt is to be preferred, again reinforced with a low shrub layer if crops alternate with grazing by stock.

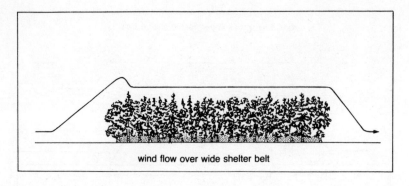

wind flow over wide shelter belt

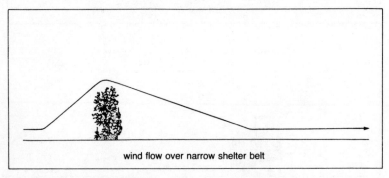

wind flow over narrow shelter belt

Fig. 15.2 Wide and narrow shelter belts.

There is no need from the protection point of view to have a wide shelter belt and indeed a woodland can be less effective than a narrow belt if crops are to be sheltered or soil erosion in adjacent fields prevented (Fig. 15.2)

But there is a practical width limit below which it is difficult to manage the shelter belt over a long period of time; this is about 20 metres. If timber production and pheasant shooting are also important objectives a wider belt of up to 50 metres may be considered. On very exposed rough hill ground, trees within the belt will have a better chance of survival and management will be easier if the belt width is increased to around 75 metres.

To shelter large areas parallel shelter belts are effective provided that the distance between them is no more than 20–30 times their height.

The species which may be planted successfully in lowland shelter belts are the same as those recommended for general woodland establishment on similar soils. On upland sites, where the need for shelter is usually greatest, the choice of species is

Fig. 15.3 Hedge and shrubs give a low impermeable shelter
belt for livestock. Narrow permeable belt of trees
above gives shelter to arable crops.

probably even more limited than it is for general woodland
planting in the uplands.

At the risk of some over-simplification a guide to trees suitable
for shelter belts is given in Table 15.1. As with other types of
woodland it is always worth having a look to see which species are
growing well in the locality on similar sites to those to be planted.

In addition to those listed poplars are quick growing and may
have a place where speed of growth is desired. It is worth getting
advice as to which of the many available species to use for a
particular site.

Species tolerant of relatively dense shade and therefore
suitable for thickening up existing shelter belts include beech,
holly, hornbeam, western hemlock (*Tsuga*), and western red
cedar (*Thuja*). Moderate shade bearers include lime, Norway
maple, sycamore and silver fir.

To establish a shelter belt that will be effective over a long
period of time almost certainly means planting a belt at least
20 metres wide with a mixture of broadleaves and conifers with
shrubs on the outer edges. Alternatively, a single fast-growing
species like poplar or Japanese or hybrid larch may be planted
with a view to early removal of part of the crop in groups to make
room for planting long-lived species such as oak, beech and lime;
a hedge or border of shrubs should still be planted at the same

Table 15.1 Some common trees for shelter belts. (This table should be read in conjunction with the notes on individual species, Chapter 1.)

	Upland	Upland severe exposure	Coastal	Fresh or moist soils	Dry soils	Chalk	Acid peat
Broadleaves							
Alder	•			•			
Beech	•			•	•	•	
Birch	•			•	•		
Cherry (wild)				•	•	•	
Lime	•			•	•	•	
Oaks–English	•		•	•			
–Sessile	•	•	•	•	•		
Rowan	•		•		•	•	
Sycamore	•	•	•	•	•(1)	•	
Conifers							
Noble fir	•	•		•	•		
Pine–Scots	•	•			•		
–Corsican			•(4)		•	•	
–Lodgepole	•		•	•	•		•
Larch(2)	•			•	•		•(3)
Sitka spruce	•	•		•			•

(1) If it can get its roots down.
(2) European is less suitable than Japanese or hybrid for shelter belt planting except in the lowlands on good soils.
(3) Japanese.
(4) Variety Austriaca is even more hardy.

time as the first crop. Where site conditions are such that only the most hardy conifers will grow it is still a good idea to have a mixture of species such as Sitka spruce and Scots or lodgepole pine; later on it may be possible to introduce some rowan or sycamore for diversity.

Subsequent management should follow the selection system principle of felling small groups or even single trees, and replanting so as to provide continuous cover.

One or two rows of fast-growing species like poplar or the hybrid Leyland cypress may give a quick and effective shelter belt but the trees will come to maturity at some time and have to be replaced by clear felling the lot: a selection system of management to provide continuous cover is just not practicable with narrow belts of trees.

If their layout and specification meet with approval, the Ministry of Agriculture in England and Wales and the Department of Agriculture and Fisheries for Scotland give grant-aid towards the cost of establishing shelter belts. The grant is based on a proportion of the actual costs and not, as in Forestry Commission grants, on a flat rate.

16 Uses of Wood on the Farm

Fencing

The phrase 'fence posts' as used here includes stakes, posts and strainers.

Perhaps the most obvious use for timber grown on the farm is for fencing. While many species will make a satisfactory fence, some are more suited than others in that they will last longer or are stronger.

The only British timbers that will give a service life of more than 20 years in contact with the ground (i.e. stakes, posts, struts and strainers) are oak, sweet chestnut and larch. To give this service all three must have a high proportion of heartwood, which in these three species is readily distinguished from sapwood by its much darker colour. The sapwood of all three species is unlikely to last more than three to five years in the ground.

Species that will last for more than 10 years in the ground are western red cedar, sequoia, yew and the cypresses.

All other species to be used as fence posts or struts should be treated with a wood preservative. If properly treated most will last for 20 or more years.

Although certain species are difficult to impregnate with a wood preservative, round timber (and especially that from young trees) contains an outer band of sapwood which is less resistant to the penetration of the preservative. Extensive tests in different parts of the country have shown that properly treated round fence posts give as good a service life or better than traditional sawn or cleft posts of oak or sawn larch posts.

Of the more commonly grown species the following are resistant to penetration by wood preservatives; the sapwood is always more easily penetrated than the heartwood which is the basis of the classification:

Cherry	Douglas fir
Oak	Larches
Poplar	Spruce
Sweet chestnut	Western red cedar
Willow	Yew

The following will accept wood preservatives with relative ease:

Alder	Hornbeam
Ash	Lime
Beech	Sycamore
Birch	Pines
Horse chestnut	Silver firs

Preservative treatment of round posts on the farm

Round material for fencing posts should be felled in the winter, the bark removed, then cut to the desired post lengths, pointed and cross-stacked to dry in a weed-free exposed place to allow the maximum amount of wind to blow through the stack. They will then be ready for preservative treatment by the summer (Fig. 16.1).

An old oil drum filled about one-third full of creosote, placed on bricks over a wood fire, should be heated till the creosote is hot. The posts are then inserted in the hot creosote points down and the fire maintained for three hours during which time the air in the posts expands and bubbles out through the creosote, then the fire is extinguished or left to die out. Creosote expands as it is heated and it is highly flammable, so it is important not to overload the drum with stakes; the (hot) creosote level should be kept 15 cm (6 inches) below the top rim of the oil drum. The whole operation should be carried out well away from buildings and flammable material. The drum and the posts are left to cool overnight to draw the creosote into the posts as the air in the wood tissue contracts. Next morning the fire should be re-lit and the creosote re-heated for another three hours to drive out surplus creosote. The posts are then removed from the hot creosote and stacked to dry or the process may be started again, this time treating the top half of the post.

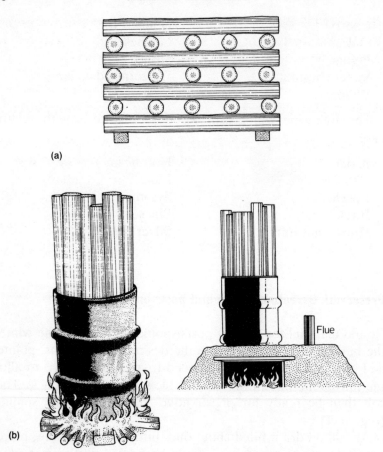

(a)

(b)

Fig. 16.1 (a) Posts piled for drying. (b) Improvised
creosoting plant. Enclose the fire for safety and
provide flue.

An alternative is to have a second drum of cold creosote into
which the hot posts are placed after their first three-hour heating
in the hot creosote drum and left overnight to absorb the
creosote.

Half-round and quartered posts can be similarly treated,
although the heartwood will absorb less creosote. Sawn timber of
the easily treated species listed above can also be so treated for
use in contact with the ground.

For longer pieces of wood a rectangular tank is needed, handling
is more difficult, and the timber may need to be weighted down in

the tank. On balance it is probably more cost-effective to have the timber treated in a commercially operated pressure plant using creosote or a copper-chrome-arsenic preservative.

Natural durability and ease of treatment with a preservative

The suitability of the most common species of timber for fencing and the necessity for treatment with a wood preservative are summarised in Table 16.1.

Table 16.1 The necessity for treatment of fences with wood preservatives by species and components.

Timber species	Round posts	Half-round posts	Half-round rails	Sawn posts	Sawn rails
Alder	PTE	PTE	PTD	PTE	PTD
Ash*	PTE	PTE	PTD	PTE	PTD
Beech	PTE	PTE	PTD	PTE	PTD
Birch	PTE	PTE	PTD	PTE	PTD
Cherry	PTE	PTE	PTD	PTE	PTD
Hornbeam	PTE	PTE	PTD	PTE	PTD
Horse chestnut	PTE	PTE	PTE	PTE	PTE
Oak*	PTE	PTE**	PTD**	UN	UN
Poplar	NR	NR	PTD	NR	PTD
Sycamore	PTE	PTE	PTD	PTE	PTD
Sweet chestnut*	UN	UN	UN	UN	UN
Willow	NR	NR	PTD	NR	PTD
Corsican pine	PTE	PTE	PTE	PTE	PTE
Douglas fir	PTE	PTE	PTD	PTE	PTD
Norway spruce	PTE	NR	PTD	NR	PTD
Larch	PTD**	PTD**	UN	PTD**	UN
Lodgepole pine	PTE	PTE	PTD	PTE	PTD
Scots pine	PTE	PTE	PTD	PTE	PTE
Sitka spruce	PTE	NR	PTD	NR	PTD
W. hemlock	PTE	PTE	PTD	PTE	PTD
W. red cedar	UN	UN	UN	UN	UN

PTE = Preservative treatment essential
PTD = Preservative treatment desirable
UN = Treatment unnecessary
NR = Not recommended for this use regardless of treatment.

Note: The charring of stakes does not increase the service life.

* Ash, oak and sweet chestnut are sometimes cleft instead of being sawn.
** If there is a high proportion of heartwood, need not be treated.

Other uses for round timber on the farm

In some areas sweet chestnut coppice is in demand for hop poles because it gives a straight strong pole of high natural durability and being available locally is cheap to transport to the hop fields. Both sweet chestnut and hazel coppice rods (which grow straight and in a range of quite small suitable diameters) can be used for the support of climbing crops such as peas, beans and vines. In areas where raspberries are grown there is a large demand for posts and struts to carry the wires which support the growing canes. The more durable types of timber can be set in the ground as fenders to buffer the corners and portals of farm buildings against damage by vehicles and machinery.

A further use is in the erection of pole barns; these are buildings where the main vertical structural support is provided by long poles set in the ground. Typically the poles have a mid-diameter of about 200 mm, and are from 6 to 10 m in length. Corsican pine (which is permeable to wood preservatives and is of good cylindrical shape), larch and Douglas fir (which should have their natural resistances to decay improved by treatment with an appropriate preservative) are the best species for pole barns. Scots pine is also suitable, but the spruces should be avoided on account of their poor retention of preservative, (techniques are available for the efficient preservation of spruce but they are not widely practised in the UK). Details of the design and construction of pole barns may be obtained from the Timber Research and Development Association, Hughenden Valley, High Wycombe, Bucks HP14 4ND (*tel:* 0240 0243091) on a fee-paying basis.

Sawn timber for general estate and farm work

Practically every species of sawn timber can be used for outdoor jobs such as portable buildings, barn repairs, gates and cribs, but some will serve better than others. Larch, sweet chestnut, oak (selected for a low proportion of the less durable sapwood), Douglas fir and western red cedar might not require preservative treatment, but most other species will. Some species such as larch, Douglas fir and sycamore are liable to split when being nailed, and preboring of nail-holes is desirable; other species such as poplar and willow need a flat-topped nail (other nails have a tendency to 'pull through'). Galvanised nails should be used with oak, sweet chestnut and western red cedar to avoid discoloration and corrosion round the nail.

Properties of the individual timbers

The properties of the various species are given below. It must, however, be emphasised that a use does not constitute a market, and while a particular type of timber may be very suitable for a specific purpose a demand may not exist. On the other hand some species are of special value. Thus although they may be well suited for farm or estate work it is often worth inviting offers for good quality logs of the following timbers even though only a single (large) tree may be involved.

Timber	Ultimate uses
Ash	sports goods, tool handles, veneers
Cherry	cabinet work, veneers
Laburnum	turnery
Oak	furniture, coffins, veneers
Poplar	veneers for vegetable crates
Robinia	cabinet-making, veneers
Sycamore	furniture, musical instruments, veneers
Walnut	furniture, veneers, gun stocks
Yew	furniture, veneers, turnery

In the list below, where the wood properties of related species are virtually identical, they are grouped under the same head. For example, 'larch' embraces European larch (*Larix decidua*), Japanese larch (*Larix kaempferi*) and their hybrid (*Larix eurolepis*); similarly 'silver fir' covers the European species (*Abies alba*) and two Canadian species (*Abies grandis* and *Abies noblis*). In both of these examples the variability of wood properties between the species is less than the variability within the species, hence for practical purposes they can be regarded as the same timber.

A further point to note is that the properties of the sapwood are usually different to those of the heartwood of the same timber. Heartwood is more resistant to attack by fungi and insects, but more difficult to treat with wood preservatives than the more permeable sapwood.

Properties of broadleaves (hardwoods)

Alder (*Alnus* spp. mainly *A.glutinosa*)

A useful medium density hardwood with moderate strength properties, but with no outstanding features. It works, nails and screws well, and is permeable to wood preservatives. When treated is suitable for fencing and estate work, and it can be used as a substitute for softwoods in the construction and repair of buildings. Good quality poles and logs are sometimes purchased by turneries.

Ash (*Fraxinus excelsior*)

One of the most useful British hardwoods, and high quality logs are nearly always in demand by hardwood sawmillers (coppice-grown material is sometimes preferred). Its resistance to shock-loading makes it the first choice for the framework of vehicles, for tool handles and sports goods, but selection is required to exclude the weaker wood. It is permeable to wood preservatives.

Beech (*Fagus sylvatica*)

One of our strongest timbers, which works, nails and screws well. It is not resistant to decay, but is easily impregnated and when treated with preservatives can be used for fencing and estate work. It is regarded as an all-purpose hardwood, but is particularly suitable for flooring, and it is favoured for small tool handles and for mallet heads. Widely used in the furniture industry.

Birch (*Betula* spp.)

A hard tough timber with good strength properties. Used in furniture-making in the Scandinavian countries and in Finland for plywood manufacture. An excellent turnery wood–large quantities of birch 'squares' were at one time imported into Britain for this purpose. British-grown birch is still in use as a turnery wood. Takes preservatives well and fence posts impregnated with creosote in the open tank process have lasted well.

Cherry (*Prunus avium*)

A timber of moderate strength properties, which works and finishes well. It is resistant to penetration by wood preservatives, hence if used for estate purposes it should only serve in situations clear of the ground. It is particularly suitable for internal joinery and furniture repairs.

Hornbeam (*Carpinus betulus*)

This is the strongest and hardest of our native woods, but otherwise it has no outstanding features. Because of its high resistance to abrasion it makes a superb floor for workshops. It is permeable to wood preservatives and is therefore suitable for estate work and fencing.

Horse chestnut (*Aesculus hippocastanum*)

A soft white wood which is virtually all sapwood and therefore perishable. It has low strength properties, and is best avoided for load-bearing situations. As it is available in wide boards it is useful for shelving in dry places, but in moist environments surface moulds may occur. It is permeable to wood preservatives, and when treated may be used out of doors, but stronger species are usually preferred for most estate work.

Lime (*Tilia* spp.)

A soft wood with a fine uniform texture which has made it a favourite with wood carvers. A good turnery wood. Used for frames for beehives and parts of musical instruments, e.g. pianos. Permeable.

Oak (*Quercus robor* and *Q. petraea*)

The outstanding properties of oak are resistance to decay and hardness. Strength properties other than hardness are moderately good, but lower than those of beech, birch and ash. The proportion of sapwood in sawn oak can be high, and where this is so preservative treatment may be required. It is suitable for all types of fencing (a service life of more than 20 years can be anticipated from untreated sawn oak posts which have been selected for absence of sapwood). Its resistance to abrasion ensures its suitability for flooring. Its ornamental effect can be exploited for internal uses such as joinery and furniture repairs.

The properties of the less common oaks such as red oak (*Q. rubra*), holm oak (*Q. ilex*) and Turkey oak (*Q. cerris*) are quite different and generally inferior.

Poplar (*Populus* spp.)

Although a relatively weak low-density timber, poplar has three advantages–a clean off-white colour, a non-splintering surface, and low flammability. The clean appearance together with the absence of any taints makes it most suitable for use in contact with food; consequently it is favoured for boxes, crates and storage shelves. However, when used for such purposes it is important to use flat-top nails for the fixing–slender nails such as panel-pins tend to 'pull through'. Its low flammability means that it is a preferred material for use in situations (such as oast houses) where the fire hazard is high; and its non-splintery nature makes it useful for the floors of waggons (it is not recommended for the floors of horse boxes and cattle trucks because the risk of decay is too great–a durable timber such as sweet chestnut or larch should be preferred).

Sweet chestnut (*Castanea sativa*)

This timber has a combination of properties which make it a most useful species for estate purposes. The heartwood is resistant to decay and the proportion of the less durable sapwood is low, hence it is an ideal material for fencing without the necessity of preservative treatment. Apart from a tendency to split and shear, the wood has moderately good strength properties. It works well giving a good finish, but it may be necessary to pre-bore nail holes. It has proved to be particularly suitable for external joinery such as window frames, glazing bars and mullions.

Coppice-grown poles are widely used for fencing (especially cleft pole fences) and in some localities it is in demand for hop poles.

Sycamore (*Acer pseudoplatanus*)

Sycamore has moderately good strength properties coupled with a clean white appearance; it works easily giving a better finish than most other timbers; it is necessary to pre-bore nail holes to minimise the possibility of splitting. It is permeable to wood preservatives, and when effectively treated can give many years' service in contact with the ground. It can be used for all estate purposes and for building work. Because of its clean colour and because it is odour-free, it is a preferred species for use in contact with food, and it is especially suitable for kitchen implements, draining boards, and chopping blocks.

Willow (*Salix* spp.)

Besides its use for high class cricket bats (for which *Salix caerulea* is used extensively) willow is used for toy cricket bats, artificial limbs, chip baskets and medicinal charcoal. Heartwood is very resistant to penetration by preservatives. Sapwood is permeable. The coppice-grown osier willows are used to make baskets, chairs and other woven-willow furniture.

Properties of conifers (softwoods)

Corsican pine (*Pinus nigra var. calabrica*)

Corsican pine is a general purpose softwood which has a high proportion of sapwood. The logs are normally straight and fairly cylindrical and are thus among the most suitable for the construction of pole barns provided that they have been treated under pressure with a preservative (pressure treatment requires special equipment and needs to be undertaken by a contractor). Preservative treatment (which may be with creosote by open tank) is also essential where this species is used for fencing and other estate work. Because of the depth of penetration of the preservative, and because of its cylindrical shape Corsican pine makes excellent posts for the support of field gates. It is rather more difficult to air-dry than other coniferous timbers, and during the late autumn and winter it is actually hygroscopic and may take up some moisture.

Where it is used for load-bearing purposes, care must be taken to avoid pieces with large knot clusters. There is no provision for its use under the Building Regulations and the local authority should therefore be consulted before it is used for structural purposes in dwellings; on the other hand there is no objection to the use of selected material for joinery. Air-dried Corsican pine sawn timber should always be stored under cover because rewetting by rain can result in the development of unsightly stains caused by fungi.

Douglas fir (*Pseudotsuga menziesii*)

Douglas fir is a good general purpose softwood with somewhat variable strength properties. It is relatively difficult to treat with preservatives, but the heartwood has some natural resistance to decay, and the sapwood will accept sufficient preservative. Hence, round or sawn timber which has been treated under pressure or by the open tank method will give adequate service when used in contact with the ground. It is well-suited for all types of fencing and estate work including the construction of pole barns. It is favoured for load-bearing purposes in building and selected wood is suitable for joinery and for flooring; for both of these purposes pre-boring of nail holes is desirable to prevent splitting.

European (Norway) spruce (*Picea abies*)

A lower density general purpose softwood in which the knots are usually small and tight. It is resistant to preservative treatment, and where it is used for estate purposes contact with the ground should be avoided. When treated, it may be used for round (but not for sawn or half-round) fence posts. It is quite suitable for rails. It is a good timber for shelving, boxes and pallet boards. In building work it can be used for structures. For joinery and flooring there might be some tendency to give a woolly finish, otherwise it works and nails well.

Larch (*Larix decidua, L. kaempferi* and *L. eurolepis*)

Larch is heavier, harder, stronger and more durable than most other softwoods, and it has become the traditional material for fencing and estate work. The heartwood of mature larch will serve for 20 years or more. If a proportion of heartwood is present, e.g. in round posts, it will usually serve for over a decade, but if treated under pressure it can be expected to last for more than 25 years.

It can be used indoors, but a tendency to distort, to exude resin and to split around nail holes, and the presence of black or dead knots which fall out after seasoning, has resulted in a preference for other species for structures, flooring and joinery. On the other hand it is particularly useful in situations such as horse boxes and cattle trucks where the risk of decay is high.

Lodgepole pine (*Pinus contorta*)

This species has much the same properties and uses as Scots pine but it is less apt to shrink and swell during changing humidities, and it gives an even better finish; it is therefore excellent for joinery, flooring and furniture if straight logs with relatively small knots can be obtained.

Scots pine (*Pinus sylvestris*)

Scots pine was until recent times the most widely used of all British-grown softwoods, and consequently it has become the yardstick against which other species are assessed. It has moderately good strength properties, is permeable to preservatives, and is easy to work and nail giving a fine finish. However, the knots are larger than in most other softwoods, and they sometimes loosen and fall out to give unsightly knot holes. It can be used for practically any application; when treated with preservative for fencing, estate work and pole barns; and indoors for structures, flooring and joinery. If used for structural work, wood with large clusters of knots should be avoided.

Silver fir (*Abies alba, A. grandis,* and *A. noblis*)

Silver firs resemble spruce and can be used for similar purposes; there are nevertheless three salient differences. They are more permeable to preservatives, and treated wood is likely to give better service when used out of doors; they have a lower resistance to impact loading and are possibly less suitable for use as pallet boards unless the thickness be increased; and when planed and sandpapered they give a less woolly finish, consequently they are preferred for the repair of kitchen furniture (they have good nailing properties).

There is no provision for the use of silver firs for structural purposes under the Building Regulations.

Sitka spruce (*Picea sitchensis*)

Sitka spruce is virtually indistinguishable from European spruce, but there is an important difference affecting its utilisation; namely it has almost invariably a significantly lower proportion of sapwood. Commonly the radial thickness of sapwood in Sitka spruce is only a few millimetres; this means that it is difficult to obtain an adequate loading of preservatives for use in contact with the ground. The timber works well and has good nailing properties, but is apt to give a woolly finish when planed, and is therefore best avoided for joinery. The knots are usually small and tight. It is suitable for fence rails, box and pallet repair, structures and flooring.

Western hemlock (*Tsuga heterophylla*)

This is a useful softwood with no outstanding features. It can be used in the same way and for the same purposes as Douglas fir.

Western red cedar (*Thuja plicata*)

Because of its low density, relatively low strength properties, and resistance to attack by wood-destroying fungi, western red cedar is a special purpose timber. In estate work preservative treatment

Table 16.2 Uses on the farm.

Species	Fence posts	Fence rails	Estate	Structural	Joinery	Other uses
Alder	i P		i P			Turnery, clogs.
Ash	i P	ii	i P	i D	i	Tool handles.
Beech	i P		i P	i D	i	
Birch	i P		i P		i	
Cherry					i	Furniture veneers.
Hornbeam	i P		i P			
Horse chestnut					i	
Oak	iii (3)	iii	iii	iii	i	
Poplar	i P	i			i	Floors, food containers, veneers for veg. crates.
Sweet chestnut	iii	iii	iii	i	i	
Sycamore	i P		i P			Kitchen and butchers' blocks. Musical instruments.
Douglas fir	i P	i D	i D	i	i	Gates (D).
Larch	iii (1)	iii	iii	i	i	
Pines						
Corsican	ii P	i D	i D	i	i	Round posts heavily impregnated = iii.
Lodgepole	ii P	i D	i D	i	i	
Scots	ii P	i D	i D	i	i	
Silver firs			i D			
Norway spruce	i P (2)	i D	i P	i D	i	
Sitka spruce	i P (2)	i D	i P	i D	i	
Western hemlock	i P	i D	i	i	i	
Western red cedar	i		i (1)		i (1)	Sheds, green-houses.

(1) Impregnate with preservative if much sapwood present.
(2) Small round posts with relatively permeable sapwood.
(3) Heartwood.
i = suitable;   ii = good;   iii = excellent
P = must impregnate with preservative
D = desirable to impregnate with preservative

is unnecessary, making it well suited for weather boarding, for fencing and for gates where its lightness in weight can be advantageous; but as it bruises easily, it should not be used in places where abrasion is likely. It is an excellent material for greenhouse construction and repair, and it is also useful for seed boxes. It tends to corrode unprotected steel and discoloration often occurs around nails, thus the use of galvanised or stainless steel nails, and brass screws is recommended.

A summary of the uses of timber from broadleaves and conifers on the farm is provided in Table 16.2.

17 Making a Farm Woodland Plan

Objectives

An essential first step in making any plan is to clarify the objectives and decide exactly what the aims are.

There will almost always be several objectives; these must be put in order of priority because there could be conflict between them. This will result in some, or all, of the aims not being achieved as fully as they might. For example, a plan for growing timber for maximum profit would have to be modified if landscape or nature conservation were a secondary objective, and something less than maximum profit would have to be accepted.

If applying for grant aid, it may be necessary to accept some objectives as a condition. Thus the Forestry Commission, as part of its scheme, requires that one objective is to produce a crop of utilisable timber; it is also necessary to have regard to nature conservation and amenity. If asked to do so by the Local Authority, owners must be prepared to discuss the possibility of an agreement for public access, although this does not bind the owner to enter into such an agreement. The Countryside Commission, as part of its schemes, requires that the work should be of benefit to the landscape and contribute to the public's enjoyment of the countryside.

There may be other constraints affecting a plan: e.g. if a wood is on the register of ancient semi-natural woodlands; if it is a 'Site of Special Scientific Interest'; if it is subject to a Tree Preservation Order; if it is in a National Park; or if it is in an 'Area of Outstanding Natural Beauty'. The different objectives will have different implications for management and some examples are given below.

Objective	Implications for management
Timber for sale	High-value species, preferably fast-growing. Possibly larger woods and uniform crops.
Timber for farm use	Useful species, e.g. larch, chestnut or red cedar, for fencing stakes and rails, possibly oak for repair of old buildings.
Firewood	Establish broadleaved coppice on a rotation of say 20 years. Cut one twentieth each year.
Shelter	Choose wind-resistant species. Design wood or belt so as to avoid ever having to clear fell, i.e. use 2 or more species with different rotation lengths.
Nature conservation	Use several native broadleaves, including non-timber trees. Have a variety of ages and crop types, including coppice.
Landscape	Design the shape and size of the woods to be in keeping with the landscape. Use chiefly broadleaved species in Southern Britain.
Shooting	Site and design individual woods to give good drives. Use a mixture of broadleaved and conifer species and leave open spaces in the woods.

Survey

For planning and management purposes and also for grant applications an Ordnance Survey (OS) Sheet on the scale 1:10,000 is appropriate (for very small areas 1:2,500). OS sheets are expensive, but they will last a long time.

Photocopies can be used for field work, keeping the master map clean and dry indoors. The basic units of management are the compartment and the sub-compartment. A compartment is a geographical entity, such as a whole wood. A very large wood might be divided into two or more compartments using a recognisable feature such as a road or a stream as the boundary. Compartments are usually numbered serially starting at the west side of the map.

Within a compartment there may be several different crops: for example, Compartment 2 may have a total area of 8 hectares of which 5 hectares is old oakwood, 2 hectares is ash coppice and 1 hectare is a young Norway spruce plantation. The different crops are recorded as sub-compartments and are designated 2a, 2b and 2c. Sub-compartments do not have permanent boundaries. On the map the external boundaries of woods are marked by a heavy line inside the boundary. Boundaries between compartments are marked by a dash/dot and sub-compartment boundaries by a simple broken line. Compartment numbers are shown in half-inch diameter circles, the number in the upper half and the compartment area in the lower.

Areas of compartments and sub-compartments can be measured from the map using a hectare grid. On grant applications to the Forestry Commission the areas are usually checked with a planimeter before the application is approved.

Choosing sites for new plantations

The objectives will influence the choice of site for creating new woods but the following are worth consideration.

(1) Ground which has been reclaimed from woodland since the War. There may have been good reasons why it was under trees previously, and woodland may be the best land use.
(2) Slopes which are too steep for cultivation. Think about how the timber will be extracted later on and perhaps leave roadlines unplanted.
(3) Wet areas. Forest drainage by open ditches could make them suitable for trees.
(4) Sites on less fertile soil, but avoid shallow soils over rock.
(5) Sites which will give shelter to buildings or livestock. When providing shelter for stock do not put plantations on exposed hilltops, where the trees will not grow well. Site such shelter belts or woods below the top, out of the worst wind in positions where the stock can move to find shelter when required.
(6) Sites where the plantation fences will help to divide up fields or hill grazing.
(7) Sites where woodland will enhance the landscape. When planting on a hillside, go down to the main road, or wherever

else it can be seen from, and try to imagine what it will look like. Try sketching it in on a photograph.

Compartment notes

As an aid to planning it is useful to make notes about each compartment. These can include features of the site (e.g. slope, soil, aspect) the existing vegetation or tree crop, anything about the past history of tree crops (e.g. when thinning or felling was done, or damage caused), what you hope to grow there, and what will have to be done to achieve the desired tree crop (e.g. drainage, herbicide application, thinning, selective felling, etc.).

Dealing with neglected woodland

Many farm woods are neglected, and there is a temptation to clear fell and start again. But clear felling means the loss, for several years, of a feature of the landscape, a source of shelter, a wildlife habitat, a source of firewood and possibly a pheasant covert. It is better to look carefully and see what potential the younger trees in the wood have. During the first half of the life of a tree it is concerned mainly with growing tall. In the second half it puts on the diameter growth which makes it valuable. To fell half-grown trees is to waste an asset. A careful assessment of the wood may show:

(1) Old trees with spreading crowns. These could produce seed in a good year which would regenerate the wood naturally if the ground conditions were right. Think about their timber quality and size, how vigorous they are and how long they have got before they start to deteriorate. Plan to fell them before that happens. There is no point in holding on to poor quality timber.

(2) Smaller trees, possibly younger. If these have a reasonable crown of branches they will respond to being given more space, and will increase in diameter and in value. If the crowns are very small and cramped, there is not much hope for them and they might as well be felled.

(3) Younger pole-sized trees, often crowded together, where there are gaps in the tree canopy. Look for straight vigorous

stems among these. If there is at least one every 8 to 10 metres there is a potential final crop of timber trees which can be brought on by careful thinning.

(4) Tree seedlings and young saplings. If these are of useful timber species they are worth looking after, because they have several years' start on anything that is yet to be planted. They will need protection from livestock and rabbits, possibly some thinning out to reduce competition, and probably more light from above.

(5) Coppice which has gone beyond its normal cutting age. If this is of a timber species it can be singled out to one stem on each stool and grown on as a high forest timber crop.

(6) Old trees with a lot of space between them and a thicket of brambles underneath. There is not much hope of natural tree seedlings coming through this. Possible courses of action are:

   (a) Spray the bramble with herbicide, then plant. The brambles may remain for several years like a barbed wire entanglement.

   (b) Plant in tree shelters at wide spacing and spray herbicide immediately round each. (If the spacing is more than 3.0 metres, the full grant may not be paid.)

   (c) Clear the bramble with a swipe, or something similar, and plant.

   (d) Run pigs in the wood. They will achieve a good clearance and a degree of surface cultivation which would help natural regeneration in a good seed year. (But they will attack the trees when easier feed runs out!)

(7) A full crop of old trees and not much else. Plan to regenerate the wood by stages within the remaining economic lifespan of the crop, e.g. by felling groups of trees every five years over a period of 25 years, taking one-fifth of the area of the wood each time.

Timing the work

Forestry plans of operations are usually made for five year periods, and the rate at which you work will depend on the resources, either of labour or of money. Maintenance work will build up as planting progresses. Planting one hectare a year gives five hectares to maintain by the end of the fifth year, and this might be more than the farm labour can cope with. More farm plantations have failed through neglect of weeding than from any other cause. List the work which will be needed in each compartment in each year, and try to get an even spread from year to year.

It is important to think about cash flow. There is often an income from existing woods (there are very few which have not got something saleable in them) and income from grants. Forestry Commisssion grants are paid by instalments, usually the biggest part after planting, and the remainder at five-year intervals subject to satisfactory maintenance. Outgoings may include the cost of plants, herbicides, fencing material, possibly purchase of tools and equipment and possibly hire of contract labour or machinery if they cannot be provided from the farm's own resources in slack periods. The total of these costs may exceed the first instalment of Forestry Commission grants so there could be a cash flow problem in the early years after planting.

Gaining experience

It is helpful to join a forestry society (address in Appendix 5). Local sections organise excursions to interesting woodlands, and the newcomer to forestry can learn much from the example and discussion on these occasions.

Appendix 1
Some Fencing Specifications used in Crofting Counties

[This extract refers to traditional mild steel wire fences and does not include high tensile wire fences.]

A. Materials and minimum dimensions

1. **Timber** shall be sound and well seasoned. Mature European larch or oak may be used untreated. All other timber must be barked and thoroughly pressure-treated with an approved preservative.
2. **Straining posts** at least 2100 mm long and 175 mm diameter at top; if sawn, 150 mm × 150 mm. Railway sleepers and telegraph poles (not less than 175 mm diameter) of good quality may be used.
3. **Turning posts** at least 2100 mm long and 150 mm diameter at the top.
4. **Struts** at least 1800 mm long (2260 mm long for high tensile fencing with droppers) and minimum 100 mm diameter; if sawn 100 mm × 100 mm.
5. **Stobs** at least 1500 mm long and 75 mm × 75 mm or 175 mm diameter quartered or 75 mm diameter at the top if round or 4500 mm^2 at the top if any other shape.
6. **Long stobs for deer fences** 2400 mm long and 75 mm × 75 mm or 175 diameter quartered or 75 mm diameter at the top if round.
7. **Droppers** 60 mm longer than the distance between wires to be covered and at least 38 mm × 32 mm. (If droppers are of metal they shall be of approved design.)
8. **Long stakes for guard wire fences at dykes** 2280 mm long and 63 mm diameter at top.

9. **Wire** shall be galvanised mild steel wire of a minimum diameter of 4.00 mm.

10. **Barbed wire** shall be two-ply 2.50 mm galvanised mild steel wire, or 2.36 mm oval section galvanised mild steel wire, each with 4 point barbs spaced at intervals of 85 mm.

11. **Woven wire** shall be made from galvanised mild steel wire.

    Heavy pattern (known as style B) shall have top and bottom horizontal wires of 4.00 mm intermediate horizontal wires and vertical wires of 3.00 mm.

    Medium pattern (known as style C) shall have top and bottom horizontal wires of 3.15 mm intermediate horizontal wires and vertical wires of 2.50 mm.

    1.15 m *roll* shall have 8 horizontal wires with vertical wires spaced 300 mm apart.

    900 m *roll* shall have 6 horizontal wires with vertical wires spaced 300 mm apart.

    800 mm *roll* shall have 8 horizontal wires with vertical wires spaced 150 mm or 300 m apart.

12. **Rabbit netting** shall consist of galvanised wire netting of No. 18 1050 mm wide 31 mm mesh.

13. **Staples** at strainers and stobs shall be galvanised mild steel 40 mm × 4 mm, and at droppers shall be 25 mm × 2.65 mm.

14. **Ratchet winders** (or raidisseurs) shall consist of mild steel straps 44 mm wide; fitted with 25 mm steel spindle and ratchet device, the whole galvanised after manufacture.

15. **Posts for post and rail fences** shall be at least 1650 mm long and 75 mm × 75 mm sections.

16. **Rails for post and rail fences** shall be not less than 75 mm × 38 mm.

17. **Gates** shall be soundly constructed of wood or steel with suitable fittings for hanging and latching. Wooden gates shall be 1050 mm high and metal gates 990 mm high before hanging. Metal gates which are not galvanised shall be given two coats of paint.

B. Erection

18. **Straining posts** shall be securely set not less than 900 mm in the ground and shall be placed at ends and corners of

fencing, at each acute variation of level and at intervals of not more than 200 m on straight lines.

19. **Turning posts** shall be securely set not less than 900 mm in the ground and placed at changes of direction of fencing.

20. **Struts** shall be fitted to all straining posts in the direction of each line of fencing secured thereto. The ends below ground shall rest on a base plate.

21. **Stobs** shall be placed at required centres and driven into the ground for a depth of not less than 450 mm.

    Long stobs for deer fencing and posts for post and rail fencing shall be driven into the ground for a depth of not less than 600 mm.

22. **Droppers** shall be securely attached to each wire and kept clear of ground and shall be not less than 60 mm longer than the distance between wires to be covered.

23. **Posts for post and rail fences** shall be securely set not less than 600 mm in the ground at intervals of not more than 1800 mm.

24. **Rails for post and rail fences** shall be butt jointed at ends on centres of stobs and nailed at each end and at intermediate stobs.

25. **Line wires** shall be strained tightly between straining posts. Plain wires shall be secured to straining posts and fixed to stobs by means of staples driven to a running fit. Staples for droppers shall be driven home at alternate angles. All wires shall be strained by means of a ratchet winder. Barbed wire on roadside fences shall be on the inside (that is, the field side) of the stobs.

26. **Woven wire** rolls shall be strained between strainers.

27. **Rabbit netting** shall be added where necessary to fences either buried to a depth of not less than 150 mm or lapped horizontally on the ground towards rabbit attack and kept down by earth sods spaced not more than 450 mm apart, and fastened to the supporting fence with wire not thinner than 1.25 mm or special galvanised clips.

C. Eligible types of fences

28. **Strained wire fence without droppers.** The fence to consist of from 3 to 7 line wires. Straining or turning posts to be set not less than 900 mm in the ground at each change of direction

and not more than 200 m apart. Stobs to be not more than 2100 mm apart.

29. **Strained wire fence with droppers.**
    (a) The fence to consist of from 3 to 7 line wires. Straining or turning posts to be set not less than 900 mm in the ground at each change of direction and not more than 200 m apart. Stobs to be at intervals of not more than 2700 mm with one dropper in between.
    (b) As for (a) but with stobs at intervals of not more than 3600 mm with two droppers in between.
30. **Woven wire fence.** The fence to consist of medium (type C) or heavy (type B) pattern woven wire. Additional line wires may be specified as required. Straining or turning posts to be set not less than 900 mm in the ground at each change of direction and not more than 200 m apart. Stobs to be at intervals of not more than 2100 mm.
31. **Line wire deer fence.** The fence to consist of ten plain 4.00 mm wires. Straining or turning posts to be set not less than 900 mm in the ground at each change of direction and not more than 200 m apart. Stobs to be 2400 mm long set at 4 m intervals with an intermediate stob 1700 mm long. Droppers to be 1800 mm long and set between each deer post and intermediate post with one 900 mm dropper set above the intermediate post.
32. **Deer fence with netting.** The fence to consist of five plain 4.00 mm wires with No. 18 1050 mm wide 31 mm mesh rabbit netting buried to a depth of not less than 150 mm or lapped horizontally on the ground towards the rabbit attack and kept down by earth sods spaced not more than 450 mm apart and fastened to three supporting line wires. Deer netting above the rabbit netting to be No. 18 900 mm wide 100 mm mesh and fastened to two supporting wires plus the common wire between the rabbit and deer netting. Straining posts, stobs and droppers to be the same as above.
33. **Post and rail fence.** The fence to consist of three or more rails. Posts to be set not less than 600 mm in the ground at intervals of not more than 1800 mm. The height of the fence from the ground shall be not less than 1050 mm to the top rail.

Appendix 2
Wood Processing Industries: Addresses and Specifications

Address	Specifications purchased
St. Regis Paper Co. (UK) Ltd Sudbrook Mill Sudbrook Newport Gwent NP6 4XT	*(1) Pulpwood* (a) Broadleaves. 　　All species with bark. 　　Length: 2.3 m. 　　Diameters: 5–40 cm. (b) Broadleaves/conifers mixed 　　loads. *(2) Chips* 　　Broadleaved species, 　　chipped. *(3) Other* 　　Broadleaved mining timber; 　　sawlogs.
Bowaters United Kingdom Paper Co. Ltd Kemsley Mill Sittingbourne Kent ME10 3ET	*(1) Pulpwood* (a) Broadleaves. 　　Any species, fresh felled, with 　　bark. 　　Length: 1 m. 　　Diameter: 5–25 cm under 　　bark measure. (b) Conifers. 　　All species, fresh felled, with 　　bark. 　　Length: 1 m. 　　Diameter: 5–25 cm under 　　bark measure. *(2) Slabwood* 　　All species with or without 　　bark.

Shotton Paper Co. plc
Weighbridge Road
Shotton
Deeside
Clwyd CH5 2LL

(1) Pulpwood
Conifers.
90% spruce. Up to 10% other
conifers. Spruce must be in
full loads; other conifers in
separate, full, loads.
Lengths: 2.3 m or 3 m.
Diameter: min. 6 cm, max.
40 cm over bark measure.
(2) Sawmill residues
Conifers.
90% spruce. 10% other
conifers. Bark not more than
1% by weight. Moisture
content 45–55%.

Thames Board Ltd
Workington
Cumbria CA14 1JX

(1) Pulpwood
Conifers. Spruce (preferred);
Douglas fir; larch; Scots pine.
Length: 1.8–2.3 m.
Diameter: 7–35 cms.
(2) Sawlogs
Conifers. Spruce only.
(3) Standing trees
By arrangement.

Caberboard Ltd
Cowie
Stirling FK7 7BQ

A wide range of species and sizes
of:
(1) Roundwood
Conifers and broadleaves.
Peeled or unpeeled.
Length: 1.7–2.1 m.
Diameter: 5–35 cm.
Broadleaves: 1.5 to 3.0 m.
(2) Roundwood (random)
Length: 1.5–3.0 m.
Diameter: 5–35 cm.
Peeled or unpeeled.
(3) Chips
Peeled and (separately)
unpeeled.

(4) Slabwood
(5) Sawdust
Wet and (separately) dry.
(6) Shavings
Wet and (separately) dry.

Egger (UK) Ltd   *(1) Roundwood*
Grange Road   All conifers and all
Hexham   broadleaves except poplar
Northumberland NE46 4JS   and elm.
       Length: 1.8–2.0 m.
       Diameter: 5–40 cm over bark
       measure.
       (2) Slabwood
       Bundled.

Highland Forest Products plc   *(1) Roundwood*
Morayhill   Scots pine preferred.
Inverness IV1 2JQ   Length: 3 m.
       Diameter: minimum 6 cm
       over bark measure.

Kronospan Ltd   *(1) Roundwood*
Maesgwyn Farm   Any species in random
Chirk   lengths with a minimum
Wrexham   diameter of 1 inch.
Clwyd LL14 5NT   Larch and poplar must be
       kept separate.

Aaronson Bros plc   *(1) Roundwood*
Hill Village   Lengths: 5½–8 feet.
South Molton   Diameters: 3–12 inches (top).
Devon EX36 4HP   *(2) Broadleaves*
       As above but minimum length
       3.75 feet.
       (3) Other
       Also used: slabwood; wood
       chips; sawdust; shavings.

Appendix 3
Measuring Timber

Timber has been measured in cubic metres since Britain adopted the metric system along with decimal currency but the older system of measurement which it supplanted is still used by some foresters and timber merchants. This system, called 'Hoppus measurement', makes allowance for the wastage, of 'loss in conversion' when timber is squared off in a sawmill. The unit of measurement is called the Hoppus cubic foot which is equivalent to 1.273 true cubic feet. As is described below, in the metric system the volume of a log is derived from its cross-sectional area (which is based on its diameter) and its length. In the Hoppus system, the volume of a log is expressed as the volume of the square baulk that could be adzed or sawn from the log. The convention adopted in this system is that the sides of the baulk that can be obtained from a log are equal in size to one quarter of the circumference of the log. Length is measured in the usual way.

In its original usage a piece of string was used to measure the circumference of the log, then folded twice and measured against a ruler to get the 'quarter girth'. Nowadays, quarter girth tapes are calibrated to read quarter girth in inches directly. Various ready reckoners are available to read volume (Hoppus feet) for a range of quarter girths and lengths.

There are approximately 27.74 Hoppus feet in a cubic metre.

Calculating volume in cubic metres

A tree trunk or stem has the shape of a tapering cylinder and the method of calculating its volume in cubic metres is based on the well known formula:

$$\text{volume} = \pi \times \text{radius}^2 \times \text{length}$$

or alternatively:

$$\text{volume} = \pi \times \frac{\text{diameter}^2}{4} \times \text{length}$$

and where the radius (or diameter) is the average for the stem, π is a constant factor of $^{22}\!/_{7}$ or 3.14159.

The diameter of a stem of a log is usually measured in centimetres and the length is measured in metres, so to convert the diameter to metres, the formula becomes:

$$\text{volume} = {}^{22}\!/_{7} \times \frac{(\text{diameter in centimetres})^2}{40\,000} \times \text{length}$$

Those preferring a ready reckoner to a pocket calculator should buy Forestry Commission Booklet 26, *Volume Ready Reckoner for Round Timber*, published by HMSO.

Measuring diameter–felled timber

Trees are not cylinders; the diameter of the stem gets smaller as one goes up the tree. The diameter used for measuring a log is therefore the diameter at the mid-point along its length (usually called the mid-diameter). If there is a swelling at the mid-point, measure immediately above it. Measurements are 'rounded down', that is, fractions of a centimetre are ignored so that, for example, if the actual diameter is between 21 and 22 centimetres, it is recorded as 21 centimetres. Diameters may be measured with calipers, but are usually measured with a special tape called a 'rounded down diameter class tape'. These come in lengths of 1 or 2 metres (for measuring small trees) or 3 or 4 metres (for larger ones)–see Fig. A.3.1. They are marked so that when put round a log they show the diameter instead of the circumference.

The measurement is taken from the end of the ring or from the point of the hook. The numbers on the tape refer to all diameters which fall between the class lines on the tape. If, when the tape is put round the tree, the end of the ring falls between two lines, the figure in that space is the rounded down diameter. If it falls on a line between two figures, the larger diameter is recorded. The 3 and 4 metre tapes are marked on the reverse side in metres, tenths and hundredths of a metre so that they can be used for measuring lengths.

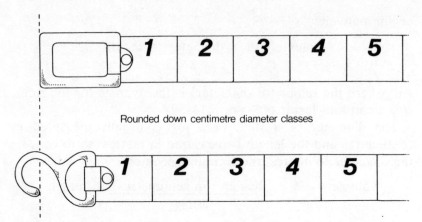

Fig. A.3.1 Metric girthing tapes calibrated to read off diameter of tree or log in centimetre classes.

Measuring length–felled timber

Lengths are measured from the butt end (i.e. the thick end) and for lengths up to 10 metres, are rounded down to 0.1 m, e.g. a stem or a log which measures 7.36 m is recorded as 7.3 m. For trees or logs of more than 10 metres the measurement is rounded down to a whole metre so that a measurement of 15.84 m is recorded as 15 metres. If the rounded down length is more than 20 metres, the tree is measured in two sections as if it had been cut into two logs. The length of the butt section is taken to the nearest whole metre below the mid-point, and the length of the top section is taken as the remainder. When measuring whole, trees the length measurement should not include anything beyond the 'timber point' (i.e. the point at which the stem is 7 cm in diameter) or beyond the point where the main stem breaks up , into branches and can no longer be distinguished (sometimes called 'the spring of the crown'). If the stem is curved, the length should be measured along the curvature and not across it.

It is often the case with broadleaved trees that the diameter of the stem changes suddenly, usually where a large branch has occurred, and in these cases the length measurement is 'stopped' at the points where the changes occur, and the tree measured in sections.

In the example shown in Fig. A.3.2, stops have been made at B and C and the tree measured in three sections:

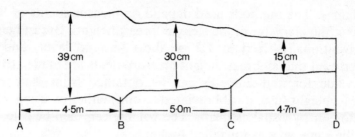

Fig. A.3.2 Dividing a log into sections for measurement.

AB–length 4.5 m, mid-diameter 39 cm, volume 0.538 cu. metres.
BC–length 5.0 m, mid-diameter 30 cm, volume 0.353 cu. metres.
CD–length 4.7 m, mid-diameter 15 cm, volume 0.083 cu. metres.

∴ Total volume of the tree = 0.974 cu. metres.

In the case of conifers the stem usually tapers gradually from butt to tip and the top of the tree is cut off at the timber point where the stem diameter is 7 cm.

In the example shown in Fig. A.3.3, the stem has been cut off at 7 cm diameter at B, and the length AB is 13.6 m. This is rounded down to 13.0 m (AC) and the mid-point is 6.5 m from the butt. The mid-diameter is 18 cm. The volume, for length 13 m and mid-diameter 18 cm, is 0.33 cu. m.

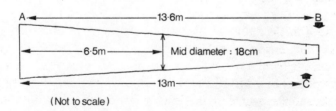

(Not to scale)

Fig. A.3.3 Taper in a conifer stem.

Measuring standing trees

Accurate measurement of standing trees from the ground can only be done using very expensive instruments. Any other methods of measurement of a standing tree can only estimate

volumes. The methods used depend on measurements of height
and of the diameter of the stem at 'breast height'. Breast height is
conventionally fixed at 1.3 m above ground level, and it is
important that all breast height measurements are made at 1.3 m.
A value for mid-diameter can be obtained from diameter at
breast height (usually abbreviated to dbh) either by using a taper
factor, or by visual estimate. The volume can then be calculated
in the same way as for felled timber.

There are other methods of getting the volume of standing trees,
and these are described in Forestry Commission Booklet 49,
Timber Measurement: A Field Guide, published by HMSO. The
methods described here are probably the easiest for a beginner.

Height

Height measurement can be done accurately by instruments using
a clinometer or a hypsometer. A reasonable estimate can be
made by using a straight stick (see Fig. A.3.4).

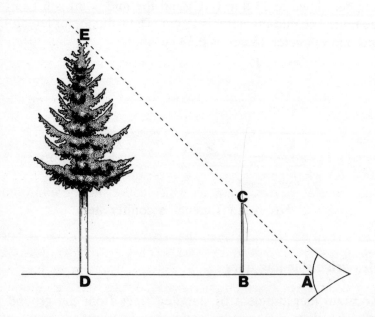

Fig. A.3.4 Estimating tree height.

Take a stick, preferably about twice as long as your arm, and hold it vertically at arm's length. Adjust your hold on the stick so that the length from your hand to the tip (BC) is the same as the distance from your hand to your eye (BA). The triangle ABC is a right-angled triangle with an angle of 45 degrees at A. Holding the stick out, move away from the tree until, without moving your head, you can align the top of the tree (E) with the top of the stick (C), and the bottom of the tree (D) with the point where you are holding the stick (B). The height of the tree (DE) is then the same as the distance from your eye to the bottom of the tree (AD) and may be estimated by pacing. There are obvious sources of inaccuracy, and the method should be practised against a known height.

For large conifers the 'timber height' (i.e. the height to the timber point, 7 cm diameter) is taken as the total height minus 3 metres.

Mid-diameter

Trees taper from butt to tip but the rate at which the diameter gets smaller varies as you go up the tree. The butt end is more cylindrical, while the top is more conical. Taper is expressed in the same way as gradient, e.g. 1:100 means that the diameter reduces by one centimetre for every 100 centimetres in length, i.e. one centimetre per metre. Individual trees vary in their rate of taper, and there are variations between species too. Average values given in Forestry Commission publications are:

1:120   for sawlogs, which are cut from the lower part of the tree.
1:84   for small wood, pitprops, etc. cut from the top of the tree.
1:100   for whole trees (except for trees grown in the open or for heavily buttressed trees which taper more rapidly than trees grown in the competition of a wood).

Here is an example of using the taper factor of 1:100. A larch tree has a dbh (diameter at breast height) of 58 cm and its total height has been estimated at 28 metres. The timber height is taken as 3 metres less than this, i.e. 25 metres and the mid-point is 12.5 metres from the butt.

The diameter at the butt is taken as the same as the diameter at breast height, and must be reduced by 1 cm for every metre of length up to the mid-point, that is 12.5 cm. The mid-diameter is then $58 - 12.5 = 45.5$ which is rounded down to 45 cm. Expressed as a formula this is:

$$\text{Diameter at mid-point} = \text{dbh} - \frac{\text{timber height}}{2}$$

The dimensions of the tree become:

length 25 metres; mid-diameter 45 cm; volume 3.98 cubic metres

(*N.B.* If this tree were being measured after felling, the length would have been measured in two sections as already described.)

Visual estimate of mid-diameter

This method may be used where a taper factor would be unsuitable and is especially useful for old broadleaved trees.

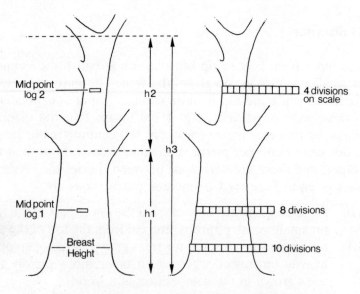

Fig. A.3.5 Visual estimate of standing tree diameters.

Figure A.3.5 shows a tree where taper factors could not be used, and an estimate of volume may be made as follows:

(1) Estimate heights h1 and h3. These are found to be 5.5 m and 10.5 m respectively. Height h2 is therefore $10.5 - 5.5 = 5.0$ m.

We have now divided the tree into log lengths as if we were measuring it on the ground.

(2) Measure diameter at breast height and estimate the positions of the mid-points of logs 1 and 2.

(3) You now need some convenient scale. This could be tenths of an inch on a ruler or the printed lines in a notebook. Move away from the tree until 10 divisions on the scale held at arm's length just covers the diameter of the tree at breast height. Move the scale up the tree and read off the number of divisions covered by the mid-diameters of the two logs. If the dbh in the example is 96 cm, the volume can be calculated as follows:

(4) Volume of log 1:
Length = 5.5 m. Mid-diameter = 8 tenths of dbh = $\frac{8}{10} \times 96$
= 76.8 which rounds down to 76 cm.
Volume for 5.5 m, diameter 76 = 2.49 cu. metres.

Volume of log 2:
Length = 5.0 m. Mid-diameter = 4 tenths of dbh = $\frac{4}{10} \times 96$
= 38.4, which rounds down to 38 cm.
Volume for 5.0 m, diameter 38 = 0.56 cu. metres.

Total volume of the tree = 2.49 + 0.56 = 3.05 cu. metres.

Measuring a stand

A 'stand' is a collective noun for a number of trees forming a wood or part of a wood.

The methods already described are satisfactory for measuring large trees, but are too slow for measuring large numbers of small trees, which may not be very valuable individually, such as thinnings. (Various methods are described in Forestry Commission Booklet 39, *Forest Mensuration Handbook*, and Booklet 49, *Timber Measurement: a Field Guide*. The one used below is also found in Forestry Commission Booklet 54, *Thinning Control*.

Briefly it consists of measuring the diameters at breast height, either of all the trees in the stand, or of a sample. An average height, called the 'top height' is found by measuring a sample of the biggest diameter trees, and an assumption about the form of the trees, or taper, is made by using a Tariff Number. Before going on to an example of this method of measurement it is necessary to look at each of these steps in more detail.

Sampling

The sample may be numerical, e.g. by measuring every third tree. Depending on the total number of trees you may need to measure a larger or smaller proportion. Below 100 trees you need to measure them all. Between 100 and 1000 trees choose a sampling fraction which will make you measure between 50 trees (at 101) and 100 (at 800 or more). Between 1000 and 4000 choose a fraction to give 100–120 measured trees, and over 4000 measure every thirtieth tree.

Alternatively, you could measure the trees on sample plots of known area. The most useful are probably 0.01 hectare (one hundredth of a hectare), a square plot 10 m × 10 m or a circular plot of radius 5.6 m, and 0.02 hectare (one fiftieth), a square plot of 14.1 m × 14.1 m or a circular plot of 8.0 m radius. Plots should contain between 7 and 20 measurable trees and you would need between 6 and 16 plots, depending on the size of the stand and whether the crop was uniform (i.e. trees of similar size and evenly spaced) or variable.

The sample trees are measured at 1.3 m from the ground using correct conventions which are as follows. The tape must be taut and at right angles to the stem. On sloping ground measure from the upper side of the tree. Leaning trees are measured at 1.3 m up the tree from the underside. Where a swelling occurs at 1.3 m, measure below it at the point where the diameter is smallest. Where the stem forks below 1.3 m treat each stem as one tree. Where the stem forks at 1.3 m measure below the fork at the smallest point. Trees of less than 7 cm diameter are not measured.

Top height

This is a technical term for the average height of the hundred trees of largest diameter per hectare, and it should not be confused with the total height of an individual tree. It has a variety of uses, among which is the determination of the Yield

Class of a crop, but we are concerned here with using it to find a Tariff Number.

Top height is estimated by putting in a series of sample plots of 0.01 ha in size, at random through the stand. The height of the tree of largest dbh in each plot is measured. If you are using plots for your girth sample measurement, the same plots will do. You need between 6 plots (for a uniform stand below 2 ha) and 16 plots (for a variable crop of over 10 ha). The tree of largest dbh is not necessarily the tallest tree.

The average of the heights measured is the top height and is, of course, rounded down if necessary to a whole metre.

Tariff number

This is a way of expressing the form of a tree.

Figure A.3.6 shows the stem form of two trees of the same diameter at breast height. The one on the left tapers rapidly and contains a lower volume of timber than the one on the right. It has a low Tariff Number, while the one on the right contains a larger volume of timber and has a high Tariff Number.

Detailed Tariff Tables are found in Forestry Commission Booklet 39 and the Tariff Numbers range from 1 to 60. If you know the average Tariff Number of your stand you can read off

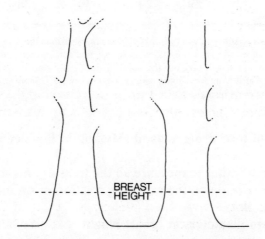

BREAST
HEIGHT

Fig. A.3.6 Tree taper and tariff numbers.

the volume for a tree of any diameter at breast height. For example–Tariff Number 28:

Dbh (cm):	10	20	30	50	70	90
Volume (cu. metres):	0.040	0.247	0.59	1.69	3.35	5.56

The higher the Tariff Number the higher the volume per tree. For example for trees of dbh 30 cm:

Tariff Number	20	30	40	50	60
Volume (cu. metres)	0.42	0.63	0.84	1.05	1.27

The most accurate way to find the average Tariff Number of a stand is to fell a range of sample trees, measure the volume of each and relate it to its dbh in the Tariff Table to find its Tariff Number. The average of the Tariff Numbers of the sample trees is the Tariff Number of the stand.

It can be estimated more quickly by using Top Height. The Forestry Commission booklets already mentioned contain tables of average Tariff Numbers for various species and Top Heights. For example the table from Booklet 54 gives the following for thinnings:

Top Height	Tariff Number						
	Scots pine	Sitka spruce	Norway spruce	European larch	Douglas fir	Oak	Birch
10 metres	18	17	18	16	16	17	15
20 metres	28	29	29	30	28	27	24

(N.B. The Tariff Numbers given in Booklet 54 are one less than those in Booklets 39 and 49. This is because the table in Booklet 54 is designed for use with thinnings. Anyone marking a thinning tends to take out the poorer trees. If Booklet 54 table is used for the whole crop the Tariff Numbers should be increased by one, e.g. Scots pine of Top Height 10 metres becomes 19 instead of 18.)

Summary of measuring a stand (Method in Booklet 54)

(1) Decide whether to measure all the trees or only a sample. If a sample, decide on the sampling fraction or on the number of sample plots.
(2) Measure diameters at breast height.
(3) Calculate the mean diameter at breast height (for method see below).

(4) Estimate Top Height and find the Tariff Number.
(5) Use the Tariff Number to find the volume of the tree with the mean diameter. (Booklets 49 and 54 have a Tariff Number Chart from which volumes can be read graphically given dbh and Tariff Number.)
(6) Multiply by the number of measured trees, and if appropriate by the sampling fraction to get the total volume.

Calculating mean dbh

To find the mean dbh you have to find the mean basal area of the stand. Imagine a tree which has been cut off at breast height. The area of the cut surface of the stump is the basal area. This can be calculated from the formula:

$$\text{Basal area} = \pi \times \frac{\text{diameter}^2}{40000}$$

or if it can be read off from the *Volume Ready Reckoner* (Forestry Commission Booklet 26) against the length for 1 metre, or from the table in Booklet 54. The basal areas of all the trees are added together and divided by the number of trees to get the mean basal area. The mean dbh is found from the mean basal area by looking in the table for the dbh which corresponds to it or by calculation from the formula.

$$\text{mean dbh} = \sqrt{\left(\frac{\text{mean basal area} \times 40000}{\pi}\right)}$$

Worked example (Method in Booklet 54)

In this example all the trees in a plot of Scots pine are being measured.

Mean basal area: $0.659 \div 19 = 0.0346$ sq. m.
Equivalent dbh falls between 20 and 21 in the table (or by calculation the dbh is 20.989 cm).
This is rounded down to *20* which is the *mean dbh*.
Top Height (average of 6 height measurements) = 16.5 m rounded down to 16 m.

Tariff No. from Booklet 54 is 24. Add 1 because total crop is being measured, so use Tariff No. 25.
Volume of tree of mean dbh 20 cm in Tariff No. 25. = 0.22 cu. metres.
Volume of stand = 0.22 × 19 = 4.18 cu. metres.

dbh class (cm)	No of trees in class	Basal area per tree	Basal area of class
11	1	0.010	0.010
14	1	0.015	0.015
15	1	0.018	0.018
16	1	0.020	0.020
17	1	0.023	0.023
19	2	0.028	0.056
20	1	0.031	0.031
21	2	0.035	0.070
22	1	0.038	0.038
23	2	0.042	0.084
24	2	0.045	0.090
25	2	0.049	0.098
26	2	0.053	0.106
Totals	19 trees		0.659 sq. m.

Bark

The thickness of the bark on a tree varies from species to species, e.g. oak has thick bark and beech has thin bark. To a timber merchant, bark is a waste product and merchants dealing in conifer sawlogs are interested only in the volume of timber under bark. To anybody selling whole trees it is easier to measure over bark and to leave the merchant to make his own allowance. Forestry Commission Booklet 39, *Forest Mensuration Handbook*, gives tables showing the amount of bark for different species and different sizes of tree.

Appendix 4
Forestry Commission Sales Agreements

Forestry Commission Memoranda of Agreement record the fact that a contract exists, the contract having been entered into when the Commission accept a tender in a sale by competitive sealed tender or a bid at Public Auction. The forms may be used after a sale by negotiation by deleting the words 'by acceptance of a tender/at auction'.

In standing sales the sale is made for the given number of trees, not the volume, because of the difficulty in guaranteeing the measurement of the volume of standing trees.

The sale is made on the basis of a single payment in advance or by instalments paid before the actual felling and removal of the trees.

In log sales the measurement may be by volume or by weighing the logs and converting the weight to volume by an agreed factor (Clause VII 2).

FORESTRY COMMISSION (FORM U29 (4/85))   AGREEMENT NO . . . .

MEMORANDUM OF AGREEMENT FOR SALE OF STANDING TREES

    I By an agreement made (by acceptance of a tender) (at auction) on . . . . the Forestry Commission acting by the Conservator of Forests for

SELLER   . . . .
    (address) . . . .
    (hereinafter called 'the Seller') agreed to sell and

PURCHASER . . . .

(address) . . . .

hereinafter called 'the Purchaser') agreed to purchase, fell and remove

THINNINGS those trees described below which have been marked by the Seller with . . . .

. . . .

. . . . and are standing on the area(s) shown by black hatching on the accompanying map

OR

CLEAR
FELLINGS those trees described below being all the trees standing on the area(s) shown by black hatching on the accompanying map

at the price and on the terms and conditions stated below and subject to the Standard Conditions of Sale attached hereto (except as regards standard condition(s) numbered . . . . which have no force or effect in the agreement) so far as the same are not inconsistent with following terms and conditions.

DURATION OF II Time is of the essence of the agreement.
AGREEMENT The operative date of the agreement shall be . . . .
and the date for completion of all work shall be . . . .

LOCATION III COUNTY [REGION] . . . . FOREST DISTRICT . . . .

DESCRIPTION IV <u>Species</u> <u>Number of Trees</u>
OF TREES
. . . .

. . . .

. . . .

. . . .

PROPERTY V The risk in all the trees standing on the area(s) shown by
AND RISK black hatching on the accompanying map shall pass to the Purchaser for the duration of the agreement. The property in those trees which the Seller has agreed to sell shall pass to the Purchaser when the trees have been paid for and felled.

PRICE VI The purchase price shall be £ . . . . plus VAT.

PAYMENT VII 1. Payment shall be made before the Purchaser starts the felling of any trees and
2. shall be made in full within fourteen days of the date of the agreement.

OR

shall be made by . . . . instalments as follows:-
a first instalment of £ . . . . to be paid not later than . . . . and . . . . subsequent

instalments each of £ . . . . to be paid not later than the following dates:-

. . . .

. . . .

The first instalment shall be deemed to be payment for . . . . of the value of the number of trees in the agreement (Each subsequent instalment shall be deemed to be payment for . . . . of the value of the trees in this agreement.)

If at any time the Purchaser has felled all the trees which he has paid for, he may if he wishes pay the next instalment before the due date and shall then be entitled to fell, remove or cut up the relevant number of trees.

INTEREST   VIII   If the whole or any part or instalment of the purchase money shall not be paid by the due date the Purchaser shall, if requested to do so, pay interest on the sum due at the rate or rates notified by HM Treasury to government departments during the period between the due date and the date of actual payment. Payment thereafter by the Purchaser will be taken by the Seller to clear the interest charged and the balance then set against the principal sum.

FORESTRY COMMISSION (FORM U30 (6/85))   AGREEMENT NO . . . .

STANDARD CONDITIONS OF SALE OF STANDING TREES

DESCRIPTION OF TREES   1. The description of the trees in the Memorandum of Agreement is believed to be accurate but the Purchaser is deemed to have satisfied himself that the number and classification of the trees is correct in all respects.

METHOD OF WORKING   2. a. All trees felled under the agreement shall be severed close to the ground and the Purchaser shall carry out the work of felling and extraction in an orderly and workmanlike manner and as work proceeds shall dispose of brushwood and lop and top to the satisfaction of the Seller and shall stack the produce as directed by the Seller. He shall take all reasonable precautions against damage to the remaining trees on the area or in any neighbouring woods or plantations or to buildings, walls, gates, fences, hedges, drains, watercourses, roads, rides and tracks and shall be liable for any damage thereto due to any act or default of the Purchaser, and shall make good any such damage.

RIGHTS OF
ACCESS

b. Rights of access using vehicles within the weight limits shown for the purpose of carrying out the agreement over the roads shown on the map attached hereto shall be given by the Seller to the Purchaser immediately the purchase price, or, where this is payable by instalments, the first instalment thereof, has been paid. No warranty is given that any other road is suitable of use by vehicles.

USE OF
ACCESS ROADS

c. All vehicles using authorised access routes shall be driven or used with all proper care and at such speed as shall be reasonable having regard to the nature of the route and vehicular load, and to the prevailing weather and road conditions. The Purchaser shall take every reasonable precaution to prevent any damage to the access routes (eg by not using them after exceptionally heavy rains or during and after a thaw, until they are suitable for use without causing avoidable damage), and shall, on request, stop the use of any machine or method of working which in the opinion of the Seller is causing, or is likely to cause, damage to standing trees or to any other property and he shall be liable for any wilful or unnecessary damage due to any act or default of the Purchaser, and shall make the same good within one week of it occurence. The Purchaser, must ensure that roads are kept unobstructed at all times and that drains are not blocked as a result of his operations.

SELLER MAY
MAKE GOOD
DAMAGE

3. In the event of the Purchaser failing to make good the damage or to dispose of the brushwood and lop and top to the satisfaction of the Seller or to stack the produce as directed by the Seller, then the Seller retains the right, two weeks after giving written notice to the Purchaser, or after such shorter time as may be reasonable if the proposed work is urgently needed, to arrange to do the work. In this event the cost shall be a debt due from the Purchaser and shall be recoverable accordingly.

ORDER OF
FELLING

4. The Seller after consultation with the Purchaser shall decide the order in which compartments are to be worked. The order of felling and removal within the compartments shall be mutually agreed before felling is to begin.

HEALTH AND
SAFETY AT
WORK

5. The Purchaser will accept full responsibility for complying with the provisions of the Health and Safety at Work Act 1974 and all other relevant Acts and regulations in respect of the work comprised in the agreement and taking place within or upon the land, access routes and other premises of the Seller. The Purchaser will adopt the safety standards relevant to forestry operations as defined and promulgated by the Forestry Safety Council, and where, in the estimation of the Seller, there is a serious breach of the safety standards (thereby creating an immediate risk of grave personal injury) the Seller reserves the

right to order the immediate suspension of further work under the agreement until remedial action has been taken by the Purchaser. Any such suspension shall be without prejudice to any other rights or remedies open to the Seller under the agreement or otherwise.

ELECTRICITY
POWER LINES
6. The Seller will be responsible for laying down the procedure to be followed when the Purchaser is working in the vicinity of any power lines in the area covered by this agreement, and the location of any such power line will be indicated on the map attached.

PEELING OF
PINE TREES
7. During the pine shoot beetle breeding season, from May to September inclusive any pine trees felled under the agreement shall be peeled or removed from the Seller's land by the Purchaser within six weeks, failing which the Seller shall have the right to do the work and recover the costs thereof from the Purchaser.

TREATMENT
OF STUMPS
8. The Purchaser shall treat with Urea or other agreed substance the stump of each conifer tree which he fells, immediately after and in any case within 30 minutes of the felling thereof. The necessary materials will be supplied free of charge by the Seller but the required treatment shall otherwise be at the expense of the Purchaser.

FIRES
9. The Purchaser shall not light fires within the forest area without the permission of the Seller and shall take all reasonable and proper precautions under the direction of the Seller to prevent and to deal with the risk of fire in the said area or adjoining ground and the Purchaser shall be responsible for any loss whatsoever through fire attributable to his negligence.

POWER SAWS
10. The Seller reserves the right to prohibit the use of power saws or any other machines on his property on a Sunday where their use would, in the Seller's opinion, contribute a nuisance to the general public or to local residents. Such prohibition shall not be regarded as justifying further changes in the terms, conditions or prices in the agreement.

ANIMALS
11. No animals, except those employed to remove trees and produce, shall be taken or allowed on the Seller's lands by the Purchaser.

CARAVANS
12. No caravans shall be brought onto the Seller's land without the written consent of the Seller.

FELLING OF
TREES NOT
INCLUDED IN
THE SALE
13. The Purchaser shall not cut down or damage any tree not included in this sale but should any such tree (being a tree not intended to be sold) be cut down or damaged by the Purchaser then the Purchaser shall pay to the Seller as agreed liquidated damages treble the value thereof and shall retain the tree.

CONDITION OF ROADS ETC

14.   The condition of buildings, walls, gates, fences, hedges, drains, watercourses, roads, rides and tracks at the beginning of the agreement as recorded on the Schedule attached hereto shall be conclusive in all questions arising from the agreement unless the Seller subsequently improves any of the said buildings, walls, etc or builds new ones in which case a record of such improvements or new works shall be made and mutually agreed and thereafter shall form part of the agreement.

STACKING AND BUILDING SITES

15.   The Seller shall make available to the Purchaser a site or sites mutually agreed for stacking the trees sold and resulting produce and for the erection of sawmills, buildings or other approved structures and no other land belonging to the Seller may be used for such purposes. No payment for these sites shall be required by the Seller during the currency of the agreement or of any agreed extension thereof but the Purchaser shall be responsible for all charges and liabilities arising from their use.

WATER

16.   Subject to all existing rights and without prejudice thereto the Purchaser may take water free of charge from the area for domestic purposes and for such other purposes connected with the felling, conversion and removal of the trees and produce sold to him as the Seller may agree.

BARK AND SAWDUST

17.   Unless otherwise agreed the Purchaser shall at his own expense either remove from the Seller's land all bark and sawdust resulting from the Purchaser's operations or shall scatter it in the felling area clear of all ditches, drains, watercourses, roads, rides and tracks.

LIABILITY

18.   The Purchaser will indemnify the Seller against any claims for loss, injury or damage occasioned by the act or default of the Purchaser in the execution of this agreement, and will, if so requested, satisfy the Seller that he has adequately insured.

FORCE MAJEURE

19.   a.   In the event of any Government regulation or departmental order coming into operation or of any Act of God, strike, lockout or other occurrence of a serious nature beyond the control of the Seller and the Purchaser taking place affecting their ability to perform their obligations under the agreement and as a result of which the felling of the trees and/or removal and sale thereof are delayed or suspended the time limit provided for in standard condition numbered 21 shall be extended for a period equivalent in working hours and conditions to the period of delay or suspension thereby caused.

FIRE AND WINDBLOW

b.   In the event of serious fire or windblow damage occurring within that part of the forest covered by the agreement the Seller or the Purchaser may terminate the agreement immediately on giving written notice to the other party, but such termination shall be without prejudice to any rights or obligations of either party which may have arisen during the, currency of the agreement. The Seller will allow the Purchaser a reasonable period after such termination in which to remove any felled trees lying on the area.

EXTENSION
OF TIME

20. a. If the Purchaser shall require an extension of the time limits laid down in standard condition numbered 21 he may give notice in writing to the Seller to this effect not less than four weeks before expiry of the agreement setting out his reasons for such request. The Seller shall have an absolute discretion whether to refuse such request or grant the same on such terms as the Seller shall think fit taking into account any increase in volume of the trees caused by extra growth and any loss due to delayed payment of any purchase money consequent on the grant of any such extension.

SUSPENSION
OF FELLING

b. If for any reason the parties agree that felling shall be temporarily suspended on any area and that the Seller shall make available to the Purchaser as a temporary measure alternative areas for felling, then where the Purchaser has paid for the trees on the original area the Seller shall calculate the price for the trees remaining unfelled and shall credit this amount to the Purchaser towards the price of trees on the alternative areas. Payment of future instalments of the purchase price due on the original area shall be deferred during the period the felling on the original area is suspended.

FELLING
AND REMOVAL

21. Subject to standard conditions numbered 19 and 20 the Purchaser shall complete the felling and clearance of all areas in accordance with the terms hereof and shall fell the whole of the said trees and remove the resulting produce and the buildings and other erections belonging to him from the Seller's lands and leave the stacking, sawmill and other sites used by the Purchaser clean and tidy and complete his other obligations to the satisfaction of the Seller within the time prescribed in Clause II in the Memorandum of Agreement.

REWARDS

22. The Purchaser shall not offer any reward, or emolument whatsoever to any person in the employment of the Seller.

NOT TO ASSIGN

23. The Purchaser shall not assign his rights under the agreement except with the consent of the Seller and upon such terms as the Seller may require.

BREACHES
GIVING RIGHT
TO TERMINATE
FORTHWITH

24. a. If the Purchaser fails to pay sums due in accordance with Clause VII and VIII of the Memorandum of Agreement, or if he commits a breach of standard conditions numbered 8, 9, or 22 the Seller shall have the right to terminate the agreement forthwith on giving written intimation to the Purchaser to this effect and any termination shall be without prejudice to any other rights or remedies open to the Seller under the agreement or otherwise.

OTHER
BREACHES

b. If the Purchaser commits a breach of any of the terms and conditions of the agreement or standard conditions other than those referred to in sub condition a. of this condition, the Seller shall have the right by written notice to require the Purchaser to remedy the matter within a specified time and if the matter complained of is not so remedied, the Seller shall have the right to terminate the agreement forthwith and any termination shall be without prejudice to any other rights or remedies open to the Seller under the agreement or otherwise.

ACTION ON
TERMINATION

25. Upon termination of the agreement whether by written notice or expiry of time, the Purchaser shall immediately cease the felling of trees and removal of felled timber under the contract but the Seller may at his discretion allow the Purchaser a further period in which to remove any timber felled before such termination. And immediately upon such termination and the expiry of any further period as aforesaid, any felled trees and any produce therefrom being in or upon the Seller's lands and the property in which is vested in the Purchaser shall vest in and become the property of the Seller together with any standing trees which have been paid for but not severed from the ground. The Seller will be entitled either to retain or re-sell said standing trees which have been paid for but not severed from the ground and said felled trees and any produce therefrom, and provided that any other claims against the Purchaser arising from the agreement have been settled, the Seller shall reimburse to the Purchaser the value of such standing trees and felled trees and produce therefrom, of which value the Seller shall be the sole judge, less all costs and losses directly and naturally resulting in the ordinary course of events, from such termination. In the event of such costs and losses exceeding the said value the Purchaser shall on demand pay to the Seller the amount by which said costs and losses exceed said value. And the Purchaser shall within six months of the termination of the agreement remove any buildings, erections or equipment which he may have placed on the area and for which an agreement to rent the land has not been made with the Seller. Should the Purchaser fail to remove such buildings,

erections or equipment within the time specified, the Seller may retain or remove and dispose of them as he thinks fit and the Purchaser shall on demand reimburse the Seller for all costs incurred in their disposal after receiving credit for any value which the Seller may place upon them.

DEFINITION   26. The term 'Purchaser' shall include his employees, his agents, sub-contractors, or assigns or the employees of any of them.

FORESTRY COMMISSION (FORM U31 (REVISED FEBRUARY 1987))

SCHEDULE TO AGREEMENT NO . . . .

The general condition of Buildings, Walls, Gates, Fences, Hedges, Drains, Watercourses, Roads, Rides and Tracks at the commencement of this agreement are recorded as follows:

FORESTRY COMMISSION (U35 (REVISED MAY 1987))   AGREEMENT NO . . . .

MEMORANDUM OF AGREEMENT FOR SALE OF LOGS BY VOLUME

I   By an agreement made/by acceptance of a tender/at auction on . . . ., the Forestry Commission acting by the Conservator of Forests for . . . . (address) . . . . (hereinafter called 'the Seller') agreed to sell and . . . . of . . . . (hereinafter called 'the Purchaser') agreed to buy those logs which are described below at the price and on the terms and conditions stated below and subject to the standard conditions of sale attached hereto [except as regards standard condition(s) numbered . . . . which shall have no force or effect in the agreement] so far as the same are not inconsistent with the following terms and conditions.

DURATION
OF
AGREEMENT

II The volume as shown in Clause V shall be made available over a period of
.... months from .... to ....

LOCATION

III The logs will be made available at ....
....
as indicated on the map attached hereto.

DESCRIPTION

IV 1. SPECIES ....
....
....

2. LENGTH

The logs shall have a minimum length of .... m
and a maximum length of .... m

3. DIAMETER

The minimum top diameter shall be .. .. cm under bark.

4. LOG CLASSIFICATION

Logs will be classified in accordance with the Forestry Commission booklet 'Softwood Sawlogs—presentation for sale'.

QUANTITY

V The approximate quantity in cubic metres measured under bark to be supplied under the agreement is as follows:-

SPECIES AND/OR SIZE CLASS	APPROXIMATE VOLUME
....	....
....	....
....	....
....	....

DELIVERY
PROPERTY AND
RISK

VI 1. The Seller shall make the logs available for collection at roadside in reasonably equal monthly quantities having regard to the effect of seasonal working conditions and holidays. Logs will be stacked at roadside in such fashion as to facilitate removal. Authority to remove each load of logs to be collected by the Purchaser shall be issued by the Seller by means of a Forestry Commission Conveyance Note. [The timber shall be collected by the Purchaser and the Seller will load the timber on to the Purchaser's transport. The Seller reserves the right to refuse to load any vehicle which he considers is unsuitable in itself or unsuitably equipped for haulage of the timber but the fact that he has loaded a vehicle shall not be deemed to indicate that he warrants the vehicle to be suitable or suitably equipped, or that the load is safely and securely stacked, or that it complies with statutory requirements]. The Seller shall notify the Purchaser from time to time of the availability of parcels of logs which need not be equal in size to one month's instalment and the Purchaser shall collect the logs so notified within three weeks of the date of notification.

2.   The Seller undertakes to permit collection of logs during normal forest working hours on Mondays to Fridays excluding Public Holidays. If the Purchaser gives adequate notice and is prepared to accept any extra costs which may be incurred by the Seller then the Seller, if he is able to do so, will permit collection outside normal hours; any extra costs to be charged will be advised when permission is given to the Purchaser to collect outside normal hours.

3.   Logs supplied pursuant to the agreement shall be at the Purchaser's risk immediately upon collection or 21 days following notification of availability as provided for in sub-clause 1 of this Clause, whichever is the sooner.

4.   Property in logs so supplied shall pass to the Purchaser when all sums due from the Purchaser to the Seller in respect of those logs have been paid in full.

MEASUREMENT   VII   1.   The volume of a log shall be calculated from the length (rounded down to the nearest 0.1 m) and the top diameter under bark using the sawlog tables set out in Forestry Commission Booklet No 31.

2.   It shall be open to the Seller and the Purchaser to agree a sample method of estimating the volume of individual lorry loads.

DEFECTS AND   VIII   No claims for defects or deficiencies will be enforceable DEFICIENCIES   against the Seller unless notified in writing within 14 days of the collection of a parcel of logs and any log or logs alleged to be defective or deficient are held for inspection by a representative of the Seller. Unless such notice has been given the passing of the risk in the logs as provided for in Clause VI shall imply agreement of the volume as notified and no adjustments or allowances will be made thereafter.

PRICE   IX   The purchase price for the logs at roadside shall be £
plus VAT per cu m
under bark for logs of .... and £
plus VAT per cu m
under bark for logs of ....

PAYMENT   X   1.   If the Purchaser is regarded by the Seller (whose discretion shall in this respect be absolute) as credit-worthy, then the Seller shall render invoices upon agreement of the volume of logs as notified and as provided for Clause VIII of this Memorandum and payment shall be made by the Purchaser in respect of each invoice not later than the end of the calendar month following the month in which the logs were collected.

2. Or if the Purchaser produces a guarantee from a clearing bank or any other institution which the Seller (whose discretion shall in this respect be absolute) regards as satisfactory for an amount no less than twice the monthly sum calculated in accordance with sub-clause 3 of this clause, then the Seller shall render invoices in accordance with sub-clause 1 of this clause.

3. Otherwise the Purchaser shall be required to make monthly payments in advance. The value of each monthly payment to be calculated by multiplying the number of cubic metres specified in Clause V of this Memorandum by the price per cubic metre (including VAT) specified in Clause IX of this Memorandum and further dividing by the number of months in the period of the agreement as specified in Clause II of this Memorandum. The Seller shall invoice the Purchaser for the sum required each month and until such sum shall have been paid the Purchaser will not be permitted to remove any logs.

FORESTRY COMMISSION (FORM U36 (REV'D 11/84))   AGREEMENT NO . . . .

STANDARD CONDITIONS OF SALE OF LOGS

METHOD OF WORKING

1. a. The Purchaser shall remove the logs in an orderly workmanlike manner and as work proceeds shall keep the logs and any debris resulting from loading operations clear of all existing buildings, walls, gates, fences, hedges, drains, watercourses, roads, rides and tracks. He shall take all reasonable precautions against damage to trees on the area or in any neighbouring woods or plantations or to buildings, walls, gates, fences, hedges, drains, watercourses, roads, rides and tracks and shall be liable for any avoidable damage thereto due to the act or default of the Purchaser and shall make good any such damage.

b. Rights of access over the routes shown on the map attached hereto using vehicles within the weight limits shown shall be given from time to time as necessary by the Seller to the Purchaser. No warranty is given that any other road is suitable for use by vehicles. The Seller reserves the right to close all or part of any such routes for such period or periods as he may determine on giving to the Purchaser reasonable prior notice.

c. All vehicles using authorised access routes shall be driven or used with all proper care and at such speed as shall be reasonable having regard to the nature of the route and vehicular load, and to the prevailing weather and road conditions. The Purchaser shall take every reasonable precaution to prevent any avoidable damage to the access routes (eg by not using them after exceptionally heavy rains or during and after a thaw, until they are suitable for use without causing avoidable damage), and shall, on request, stop the use of any machine or method of working which in the opinion of the Seller is causing, or is likely to cause, damage to standing trees or to any other property and he shall be liable for any wilful or unnecessary damage due to acts or the default of the Purchaser, and shall make the same good within one week of its occurrence. The Purchaser, must ensure that roads are kept unobstructed at all times and that drains are not blocked as a result of his operations.

SELLER MAY MAKE GOOD DAMAGE
2. In the event of the Purchaser failing to make good the damage or to keep the logs and any debris resulting from loading operations clear of all existing buildings, walls, gates, fences, hedges, drains, watercourses, roads, rides and tracks, the Seller retains the right, two weeks after giving written notice to the Purchaser, or after such shorter time as may be reasonable if the proposed work is urgently needed, to arrange to do the work and in this event the cost shall be a debt due from the Purchaser and shall be recoverable accordingly.

HEALTH AND SAFETY AT WORK
3. The Purchaser will accept full responsibility for complying with the provisions of the Health and Safety at Work Act 1974 and all relevant regulations in respect of the work comprised in the agreement and taking place within or upon the land access roads and others belonging to the Sellers, but nothing in this clause shall be deemed to impose on the Purchaser obligations or duties which are greater than those imposed by current legislation.

FIRES
4. The Purchaser shall not light fires within the forest area without the permission of the Seller and shall take all reasonable and proper precautions under the direction of the Seller to prevent and to deal with the risk of fire on the said area or adjoining ground and the Purchaser shall be responsible for any loss whatsoever through fire attributable to his negligence.

ANIMALS
5. No animals shall be taken or allowed onto the Seller's land by the Purchaser.

CARAVANS
6. No caravans shall be brought on to the Seller's land without the written consent of the Seller.

CONDITIONS OF ROADS ETC

7. The general condition of the buildings, walls, gates, fences, hedges, watercourses, roads, rides and tracks at the beginning of the agreement, recorded in the Schedule to the Memorandum of Agreement, shall in all questions arising from the agreement be taken to be evidence of the condition of such buildings, walls, gates, fences, hedges, watercourses, roads, rides and tracks. Provided that if the Seller subsequently improves any of the said buildings, walls, gates, fences, hedges, watercourses, roads, rides and tracks or builds new ones then a note of such new works or improvements shall be signed by the parties and shall be added to the agreed record so as to form part thereof.

PEELING OF PINE LOGS

8. During the pine shoot beetle breeding season, from May to September inclusive, the Seller shall have the right to peel any logs of pine which have not been removed by the Purchaser in accordance with Clause VI of the Memorandum of Agreement and to recover the costs of peeling the logs from the Purchaser.

TENANTED LAND

9. Should the Purchaser require to make use of any land in the occupation of tenants on the Seller's estate apart from any authorised access he shall himself make arrangements with the said tenants before encroaching in any way on the said land and shall indemnify the Seller from all claims in consequence thereof, but the Purchaser shall be entitled to the benefit of any conditions in the tenancy agreement so far as these tenants are concerned and should any difficulty arise over the implementation of such conditions, to have the Seller's assistance as far as possible in dealing with the tenants.

FORCE MAJEURE

10. a. In the event of any Government regulation or departmental order coming into operation or of any Act of God, strike, lockout or other occurrence of a serious nature beyond the control of the Seller or Purchaser taking place affecting his ability to perform his obligations under the agreement and as a result of which the removal and sale of the logs are delayed or suspended the agreement shall be extended for a period equivalent in working hours and conditions to the period of delay or suspension thereby caused.

FIRE AND WINDTHROW

b. In the event of serious fire or windthrow damage occurring within that part of the forest covered by the agreement the Seller or the Purchaser may terminate the agreement immediately on giving written notice to the other party, but such termination shall be without prejudice to any rights or obligations of either party which may have arisen during the currency of the agreement.

REWARDS

11. The Purchaser shall not offer any rewards, perquisite or emolument whatsoever to any person in the employment of the Seller.

NOT TO
ASSIGN
12. The Purchaser shall not assign his rights under the agreement except with the consent of the Seller.

BREACHES
GIVING
RIGHT TO
TERMINATE
13. a. If the Purchaser commits a breach of standard conditions number 4 or 11 the Seller shall have the right to terminate the agreement forthwith on giving written intimation to the Purchaser to this effect and any termination shall be without prejudice to any other rights or remedies open to the Seller under the agreement or otherwise.

b. If the Purchaser, being a purchaser in respect of whom the conditions set out in Clause X.1 of the Memorandum of Agreement are applicable, falls to pay any invoice within the agreed time as recorded in the said Clause X.1, then the Seller, in addition to the right to require by written notice payment forthwith of all sums outstanding, shall have the right by written notice to require the Purchaser to pay for the balance of the agreement in accordance with Clause X.3 or by such other method of payment as shall be determined by the Seller, and if the required payments are not then made the Seller shall have the right to terminate the agreement forthwith and any termination shall be without prejudice to any other rights or remedies open to the Seller under the agreement or otherwise.

c. If the Purchaser commits a breach of a serious nature of any of the terms and conditions of the agreement or standard conditions other than those referred to in sub-conditions a. and b. of this condition, the Seller shall have the right by written notice to require the Purchaser to remedy the matter within one month and if the matter complained of is not so remedied, the Seller shall have the right to terminate the agreement and any termination shall be without prejudice to his other rights or remedies under the agreement or otherwise.

DEFINITION
14. The term 'Purchaser' shall include his employees, his agents, sub-contractors, or assigns or the employees of any of them.

Appendix 5
Useful Addresses

Agricultural Development and Advisory Service (ADAS)
Great Westminster House
Horseferry Road
London
SW1P 2AE
(01 216 6311)

Agricultural Training Board (England)
Bourne House
32–34 Beckenham Road
Beckenham
Kent
BR3 4PB
(01 650 4890)

Agricultural Training Board (Scotland)
Overgogar House
Gogar Bank
Edinburgh
EH12 9DD
(031 339 3002)

British Association for Shooting and Conservation
Marford Mill, Rosset
Wrexham
Clwyd
LL12 0HL
(0244 570881)

British Timber Merchants' Association
Ridgeway House
6 Ridgeway Road
Long Ashton
Bristol
BS18 9EU
(0272 394022)

Country Landowners' Association
16 Belgrave Square
London
SW1X 8PQ
(01 235 0511)

Countryside Commission
John Dower House
Crescent Place
Cheltenham
GL50 3RA
(0242 21381)

Countryside Commission (Welsh Office)
8 Broad Street
Newtown
Powys
(0686 26799)

Countryside Commission for Scotland
Battleby
Redgorton
Perthshire
PH1 3EW
(0738 27921)

Department of Agriculture and Fisheries for Scotland
Chesser House
500 Gorgie Road
Edinburgh
EH11 3AW
(031 443 4020)

Farming and Wildlife Advisory Trust
The Lodge
Sandy
Bedfordshire
SG19 2DL
(0767 80551)

Forestry Commission (Head Office)
231 Corstorphine Road
Edinburgh
EH12 7AT
(031 334 0303)

Forestry Commission (N. England)
1a Grosvenor Terrace
York
YO3 7BD
(0904 20221)

Forestry Commission (E. England)
Gt Eastern House
Tennison Road
Cambridge
CB1 2DU
(0223 314546)

Forestry Commission (W. England)
Avon Fields House
Somerdale
Keynsham
Bristol
BS18 2BD
(0272 869481)

Forestry Commission (N. Scotland)
21 Church Street
Inverness
IV1 1EL
(0463 232811)

Forestry Commission (Mid Scotland)
Portcullis House
Glasgow
G2 4PL
(041 248 3931)

Forestry Commission (S. Scotland)
Greystone Park
55/57 Moffat Road
Dumfries
DG1 1NP
(0387 69171)

Forestry Commission (Wales)
Victoria House
Victoria Terrace
Aberystwyth
Dyfed
SY23 2DG
(0970 612367)

Forestry Commission Research Station
Alice Holt Lodge
Wrecclesham
Farnham
Surrey
GU10 4LH
(0420 22255)

Forestry Commission Northern Research Station
Roslin
Midlothian
EH25 9SY
(031 445 2176)

Forestry Safety Council
231 Corstorphine Road
Edinburgh
EH12 7AT
(031 334 0303)

Forestry Training Council
231 Corstorphine Road
Edinburgh
EH12 7AT
(031 334 0303)

The Game Conservancy Ltd
Fordingbridge
Hants
SP6 1EF
(0425 52381)

Institute of Chartered Foresters
22 Walker Street
Edinburgh
EH3 7HR
(031 225 2705)

Nature Conservancy Council
HQ Northminster House
Peterborough
PE1 1UA
(0733 40345)

Nature Conservancy Council
Regional Headquarters: England
Northminster House
Peterborough
PE1 1UA

Nature Conservancy Council
Regional Headquarters: Scotland
12 Hope Terrace
Edinburgh
EH9 2AS
(031 447 4784)

Nature Conservancy Council
Regional Headquarters: Wales
Plas Penrhos
Fford Penrhos
Bangor
Gwynedd
LL57 2LQ
(0248 37 044)

Ministry of Agriculture, Fisheries and Food
Whitehall Place
London
SW1A 2HH
(01 233 3000)

Royal Forestry Society: England, Wales and Northern Ireland
102 High Street
Tring
Herts
HP23 4AH
(0442 822028)

Royal Institution of Chartered Surveyors (England and Wales)
12 George Street
London
SW1P 3AD
(01 222 7000)

Royal Institution of Chartered Surveyors (Scotland)
9 Manor Place
Edinburgh
EH3 7DN
(031 225 7078)

Royal Scottish Forestry Society
11 Atholl Crescent
Edinburgh
EH3 8HE
(031 229 8180 or 031 229 8851)

Scottish Colleges of Agriculture
    ESCA
    West Mains Road
    Edinburgh
    EH9 3JG
    (031 667 1041)

    WSCA
    Auchincruive
    Ayr
    KA6 5HW
    (0292 520331)

    NSCA
    581 King Street
    Aberdeen
    AB9 1UD
    (0224 480291)

Scottish Landowners' Federation
18 Abercrombie Place
Edinburgh
EH3 6TY
(031 556 4466)

Timber Growers (UK) Ltd
Agriculture House
Knightsbridge
London
SW1X 7NJ
(01 235 2925)

Timber Growers (UK) Ltd
(Scottish HQ)
5 Dublin Street Lane South
Edinburgh
EH1 3PX
(031 557 0944)

Local offices of national government departments and agencies
are listed in local telephone directories.

Appendix 6
Glossary of Terms

Ancient woodland: Woodland which has been in existence since the Middle Ages (before 1600). The presence of wood on the First Edition of the Ordnance Survey map is evidence of this status, but not conclusively so. The wood need not consist of native trees.

Ancient semi-natural woodland: Ancient woodland consisting of species native to the site.

Basal area: The area of the cross-section of a stem at breast height (1.3 m above ground level). The basal area of a wood is the sum of the basal areas of the trees composing it.

Beating up: The replacement of plants, which have died after planting, with new ones.

Biomass crop (energy crop):   Tree species grown as a field crop, of coppice on a short rotation (up to 5 years), for the production of wood chips for fuel or pulp.

Board mills: Wood-using industries which break wood down and reconstitute it into flat uniform sized boards, e.g. building boards like fibreboard (hardboard and insulation board); wood chipboard (particle board); medium density fibreboard; oriented strand board.

Brashing: The removal of the lower branches of trees in a wood so as to make access easier.

Breast height: The standard height at which the diameter of the stem of a standing tree is measured, namely at 1.3 metres above ground level.

Broadleaves: Trees with broad, flat leaves, as opposed to needle or scale-leaves. This includes the common native species like oak and beech. Broadleaved trees are usually deciduous, but not necessarily so, e.g. holly is an evergreen broadleaf.

Canopy: The part of the wood occupied by the branches and crowns of the trees. When the branches meet so as to limit the amount of light reaching the ground, the canopy is said to be closed.

Chipboard: Wood chipboard = particle board. Board in a range of thicknesses (but commonly 18 mm) made by gluing together wood chips or particles under heat and pressure to give a sheet material very widely used for furniture, flooring, partitioning and for many other internal uses.

Chlorosis: A condition in which the leaves or needles are yellow and small, growth and vigour decline, and the tree may die. Usually occurs in conifers planted on chalk, but can occur in other circumstances, e.g. in spruces planted among heather.

Cleaning: The removal of unwanted woody species just before a plantation canopy closes.

Compartment: An area of woodland delineated on a map, and by features on the ground, forming a convenient division of a forest for management purposes.

Conifers: Trees which have needle-leaves or scale-leaves and bear cones. They are usually, but not always, evergreen. Some, e.g. larch, are deciduous.

Coppice: A type of woodland management in which trees are felled and allowed to regrow by shoots from the cut stumps, giving several stems from one root, for the production of small poles.

Coppice with standards: Coppice in which some trees (standards) are retained to grow on to produce large timber.

Cord: A unit of volume measurement for stacked wood (128 cubic feet) derived from measurement of the overall dimensions of the stack.

Deciduous: Trees which lose their leaves for part of the year, normally in winter.

Double mouldboard plough: A plough used for moorland afforestation which throws out a ribbon of turf on both sides of the furrow.

Drifts: Groups of trees of one species, planted among another species to create a mixed wood. They may be elliptical in shape but preferably irregular, longer than they are wide, and varying in size to give a natural appearance.

Even aged: A crop in which the trees are, or appear to be, all of the same age. It can result from planting or from natural seedlings arising after a felling.

Exposure: The degree to which a site is exposed to wind. It may be judged by the position of the site relative to the visible horizon. If the site is above the horizon it is exposed. If below the horizon it is sheltered.

Extraction: The operation of removing felled timber from the wood to a road accessible by lorry.

Felling: The harvesting of trees, usually for the purpose of restocking the wood. In *'clear felling'* all the trees are felled. In *'selective felling'* chosen trees are felled while others are left standing. This should not be confused with *'selection felling'* which refers to the 'selection system' of management for uneven-aged woods, in which the thinning of immature trees is combined in one operation with the felling of mature trees.

Final crop: The trees which remain after successive thinnings, and are finally felled at maturity.

Form: The general shape of a tree. Trees of good form are straight, more or less cylindrical, with fine branches, and do not taper rapidly.

Forwarder: A four-wheel drive or tracked vehicle capable of leaving a road to pick up and carry timber, and equipped with a hoist.

Fraying: The action of a deer in cleaning its antlers by rubbing against the stem of a sapling. This strips the bark from the tree, seriously damaging or killing it.

Frost hollow: A hollow in the ground where cold air collects causing damage to new shoots of trees in late spring/early summer. A similar effect can be caused if a belt of trees prevents the flow of cold air down a slope.

Gleys: Soils with restricted drainage, characterised by bluish or greenish grey mottling in the lower layers. They require draining before planting.

Ground flora: The plants, grasses, herbs, etc. growing on the forest floor.

Hardboard: Fibreboard. A sheet material commonly ⅛ inch thick made from pulped wood. Exterior grade is waterproofed.

Hardwoods: The timber from broadleaved trees. It is often, but not always, harder than the timber from conifers.

Heartwood: The wood in the centre of a tree, which is no longer in use for conducting water from the roots to the leaves. It is often darker in colour than the outer wood (sapwood) and may contain chemicals which make it more resistant to decay.

High forest: The normal system of woodland management in which trees are allowed to grow to mature size before felling (as opposed to coppice).

Hoppus foot: (= 1.273 cubic feet). An obsolescent unit of volume measurement for round timber. There are approximately 27.74 Hoppus feet in a cubic metre.

Iron pan: A soil in which iron compounds have been washed down from the upper layers and deposited as a hard layer lower down. The layer prevents free drainage and root penetration but may possibly be broken mechanically by subsoiling.

Insulation board: A thicker less dense form of fibreboard with higher insulation values than hardboard.

Light demander: A species which requires abundant light for its growth.

Matrix: A term used in describing the planting of mixed crops, in which the majority species forms a framework or matrix into which groups of the minority species are set.

Medium density fibreboard (MDF): A man-made board in which wood is reduced to pulp and the wood fibres pressed together with glue to make a flat panel. MDF is a relatively new product and has a wider range of uses, and is harder than, traditional fibreboard.

Monoculture: Growing a crop consisting of a single species. Management of such a crop is simpler, but there may be environmental disadvantages.

Oriented strand board (OSB): A form of man-made building-board in which wood is reduced to flat strands which are interlaced and glued together under pressure to produce a strong board. This has superior strength properties and is more durable than chip-board, and it is cheaper than plywood, for which it can be substituted in many uses.

Podsol: An acid soil in which aluminium and iron compounds have been washed down (leached) from the upper layers (horizons) and have been deposited in the lower ones. Generally they are coarse-textured, freely draining soils with a grey, bleached layer under the surface humus. There is a darker horizon beneath, which contains some humus above the brown iron staining.

Preparation of ground: A general term for the work which must be done before ground is fit for planting. It usually includes clearing scrub, burning up branchwood, elimination of potential weeds, ploughing or cultivation and sometimes is used to include fencing and draining. (Not all these operations may be necessary on a given site.)

Provenance: In species which have a wide geographical distribution the trees from a particular region may show characteristics (e.g. resistance to exposure) different from those of trees from other locations. These regional variations are known as provenances. Trees grown from seed of a particular provenance will always show the characteristics associated with that provenance.

Pruning: The removal of branches to improve the stem form and/or to produce knot-free timber.

Pure crop: A crop consisting of a single species (monoculture).

Regeneration: The process of replacing one crop of trees with another either artificially, by planting, or naturally, by seedlings or by coppice shoots. The term 'natural regeneration' is often applied to seedlings which have arisen naturally.

Rotation: The period of time between successive fellings. It is usually used in respect of the final crop, and will be the age at which the final crop trees are felled. *Thinning rotation* is the interval between thinnings, usually 3 to 5 years. *Financial rotation* is the final felling age which gives the best financial return.

Sapwood: The outer part of the wood of a tree which contains living cells and through which water and dissolved minerals pass from the roots to the leaves.

Scrub: Shrubby growth or trees of poor form, not capable of yielding useful produce.

Shade bearer: A species capable of surviving and growing under shade.

Shake: A defect in timber, visible after felling, consisting of cracks either radiating from the centre (star shake) or following the annual rings (ring shake), which substantially reduces its value.

Silviculture: The cultivation of woods so as to satisfy man's requirements for their products in an economical and systematic manner.

Skidder: A tractor which extracts timber by dragging it along the ground.

Snedding: (= trimming). The operation of cutting off the branches of a tree after felling.

Spring of the crown: The point at which the stem of a tree breaks up into branches so that it can no longer be distinguished.

Stand: A collective noun used for a number of trees in a wood or part of a wood.

Stool: A cut stump from which coppice shoots spring.

Sub-compartment: A sub-division of a compartment in which there is a difference in the crop which makes it suitable for different management treatment.

Tariff: A method of estimating the standing volume of a wood from measurements of diameter at breast height. Numbered *Tariff Tables* cover a range of stem forms from No. 1 (the poorest) to No. 60 (the best). The table for each *Tariff Number* gives a volume over bark for each breast height diameter. The correct Tariff Number to use for a particular stand is found by felling a sample of trees, or from measurements of Top Height.

Thinning: Cutting out some of the trees in a wood in order to affect favourably the growth and quality of those remaining. *Mechanical thinning*–thinning in which a pre-determined proportion of the trees is removed without regard to their size or quality. The method might be to remove, for example, every third tree or perhaps every fourth row of trees. The latter is called *line thinning*. *Selective thinning*–thinning in which the trees to be removed are chosen, usually so as to give maximum benefit to the trees which remain.

Timber height: The height of a tree to the spring of the crown or to the point at which the diameter of the stem is 7 cm over bark, whichever is reached first. On a felled tree this point is called the *Timber point.*

Top height: In theory, the average height of the hundred trees of largest diameter per hectare. In practice it is the average height of a sample of the largest diameter trees.

Transplant: A plant which has undergone the process of transplanting, as opposed to a 'seedling' which has not. In a forest nursery seedlings are normally transplanted after one or two years in the seed bed so as to develop a better root system and a sturdier plant.

Tree guard: A structure designed to protect an individual tree from damage by browsing animals. They range from wire-netting or plastic mesh netting tubes placed over small trees for protection against rabbits, to substantial wood or metal structures to protect trees planted in hedgerows or parkland from cattle.

Tree shelter: A translucent plastic tube, usually 1.2 m tall, which is placed over a young tree to give more rapid height growth. It also protects against rabbit damage and gives some protection against deer.

Undercut seedling: A nursery-grown seedling which has had its tap root cut by passing a blade through the seedbed a few inches below ground level. This process encourages the growth of lateral roots, and is an alternative to transplanting as a means of obtaining sturdy planting stock with bushy root systems.

Underwood (understorey): A tree crop growing beneath the main canopy and forming a distinct lower storey. It is usually of coppice but can be of planted or naturally seeded trees.

Weeding: The elimination of competing vegetation around young trees by herbicide or by cutting. When the trees are big enough to overcome weed competition the plantation is said to be established.

Weed wiper: A tool for the precise application of herbicide to weeds, while avoiding the trees. In shape it resembles a domestic broom, with a reservoir for herbicide in the handle. The head is furnished with a wick of nylon rope into which the herbicide flows at a controlled rate.

Yield class: A way of expressing the productivity of a particular crop on a particular site. It is signified by a number which represents the annual production of timber averaged over its 'economic' lifetime (or, more correctly, to the age at which the mean annual increment culminates). Thus a crop of yield class 10 produces 10 cubic metres of timber per year on average.

Appendix 7
Conversion Factors

Length

Inch	= 25.4 millimetres (mm)	Millimetre	= 0.039 inches
Foot	= 30.48 centimetres (cm)	Centimetre	= 0.0328 feet
Yard	= 0.9144 metres (m)	Metre	= 1.094 yards
Mile	= 1.609 kilometres (km)	Kilometre	= 0.621 miles

Area

Acre	= 0.4047 hectares (ha)	Hectare	= 2.471 acres

Volume

Pint (Imperial)	= 0.568 litres (L)	Litre	= 1.76 pints
Gallon	= 4.546 litres	Litre	= 0.220 Imp. Gallons
Cubic foot	= 0.0283 cubic metres (cu m)	Cubic metre	= 35.32 cubic feet

Weight

Pound	= 0.4536 kilogrammes (kg)	Kilogramme	= 2.2 pounds
Ton	= 1.016 metric tonnes	Metric tonne	= 0.984 tons

Quarter girth measurement system

Hoppus foot	= 1.273 cubic feet
	= 0.036 cubic metres (cu m)
Cubic metre	= 27.736 Hoppus feet
Hoppus feet per acre × 0.089	= Cubic metres per hectare
Cubic metres per hectare × 11.22	= Hoppus feet per acre

Planting distances/plants per hectare and per acre

Planting distance in metres (feet)	Plants/hectare	Plants/acre
1.0 × 1.0 (3.28)	10,000	4,050
1.5 × 1.5 (4.92)	4,444	1,800
1.6 × 1.6 (5.25)	3,906	1,582
1.8 × 1.8 (5.91)	3,086	1,250
2.0 × 2.0 (6.56)	2,500	1,013
2.2 × 2.2 (7.22)	2,066	837
2.4 × 2.4 (7.87)	1,736	703
2.5 × 2.5 (8.20)	1,600	648
3.0 × 3.0 (9.84)	1,111	450

Index